74768

Philliber, William W., 1943-
    Appalachian migrants in urban America
: cultural conflict or ethnic group
formation? / William W. Philliber. --
New York, N.Y. : Praeger Publishers,
1981.
    xiii, 138 p. ; 24 cm.
    Bibliography: p. 130-135.
    Includes index.
    ISBN 0-03-059687-4 : $19.95

    1. Mountain whites (Southern States)
--Ohio--Cincinnati. 2. Cincinnati
(Ohio)--Social conditions. 3. Rural-
urban migration--United States.
I. Title

08 FEB 83   7672108   OMMMsl   81-11949

APPALACHIAN MIGRANTS IN URBAN AMERICA

APPALACHIAN MIGRANTS IN URBAN AMERICA

Cultural Conflict or
Ethnic Group Formation?

William W. Philliber

PRAEGER

PRAEGER SPECIAL STUDIES • PRAEGER SCIENTIFIC

Library of Congress Cataloging in Publication Data

Philliber, William W., 1943-
    Appalachian migrants in urban America.

    Bibliography: p.
    Includes index.
    1. Mountain whites (Southern States) —
Ohio — Cincinnati. 2. Cincinnati (Ohio) —
Social conditions. 3. Rural-urban migration —
United States. I. Title.
F499.C59M836   977.1'78   81-11949
ISBN 0-03-059687-4   AACR2

Published in 1981 by Praeger Publishers
CBS Educational and Professional Publishing
a Division of CBS Inc.
521 Fifth Avenue, New York, New York 10175 U.S.A.

© 1981 by Praeger Publishers

To Susan
who makes good things possible

ACKNOWLEDGMENTS

This book would probably never have been written if it had not been for Mike Maloney. He suggested revision in my questionnaire, reviewed the manuscript, and was always willing to listen to ideas as I began to formulate them. But more than that, Mike always made me feel the book should be written. I appreciate his support and will forever remain in his debt.

Throughout the project, many other people played various roles. The undergraduate students in my research-methods class worked long and hard to help develop the research instrument and to conduct most of the interviews. Funds to collect additional interviews were made possible through an unrestricted grant from the Research Council, a grant from the Environmental Studies Program, and funds from the Department of Sociology, all at the University of Cincinnati. Grants to support my work during the summer months were received from the Research Council at the University of Cincinnati and the Research Foundation of the State University of New York. Finally, the research committee of the Urban Appalachian Council, and Phil Obermiller in particular, reviewed the original manuscript and made several suggestions which I have tried to incorporate.

CONTENTS

LIST OF TABLES

APPALACHIAN MIGRANTS IN URBAN AMERICA

1

AT ISSUE IN THE STUDY
OF APPALACHIAN MIGRANTS

At least one issue is settled in the study of people who migrated from Appalachia — there were a lot of them. In the three decades since World War II, an estimated seven million people left Appalachia either temporarily or permanently (Appalachian Regional Commission, 1979a). The net outmigration from the southern Appalachians alone during this period was more than three million people, over half of whom migrated during the 1950s. To call this migration substantial would be an understatement. For example, in the 1950s, a third of the population of the Appalachian portion of Kentucky and a fifth of the populations of West Virginia and of the Appalachian portion of Virginia left (McCoy and Brown, 1981). Today, an estimated six million people who were either born in Appalachia or whose parents were born there now live outside the region (Maloney, 1978). This migration rivals the movement of blacks out of the South and of dust bowlers to the West Coast as the significant migration of this century.

Those who left Appalachia either moved to cities surrounding the region or to cities in the Midwest and Mid-Atlantic States. McCoy and Brown (1981) documented the migration patterns out of southern Appalachia during the 1950s and 1960s. With the exceptions of Los Angeles and Tampa, the 30 cities receiving the highest number of migrants were in these two areas. For many people, these moves were shifts in two directions. First, they involved a move from rural to urban areas; these people were raised on the farms and in the small villages of Appalachia. Second, they frequently involved a move from south to north. The nature of these shifts required migrants to adjust to a variety of new demands. Greater population density meant greater noise level, more impersonal interaction, and less control over the circumstances of their environments. Job requirements shifted from outside work in farming, lumbering, mining, and road

1

construction to routinized factory work. Services such as health care and education were acquired in large, often bureaucratic, centers. Their patterns of speech
and styles of life were often different and unappreciated.

McCoy and Brown (1981) characterize these migration patterns as "streams."
People living in particular parts of Appalachia migrated to certain cities. Those
moving to Cincinnati came from eastern Kentucky. Cleveland's migrants came
from West Virginia. The migrants to Chicago and Detroit were from the coal
mining areas of Kentucky, West Virginia, and Virginia. Thus, the migrants found
in any given area perhaps have more in common with each other than do all the
migrants taken as a group.

While knowledge exists about the numbers of people who migrated and the
areas to which they moved, there is little consensus about what happened to
people once they left Appalachia. Unfortunately, the time the migration began
coincided with a decline in support for research about the region. For example,
the Russell Sage Foundation withdrew its support of the Council of Southern
Mountain Workers and of the journal *Mountain Life and Work* in 1949, after
almost a half century of support in the area, going back to its affiliation with the
work of John C. Campbell. Very few studies were conducted in the region
during the 1940s and 1950s, and even fewer were concerned with the migrants.
The gap was partially filled by the impressions of social workers and journalists,
but while perhaps accurate, they lacked the data which would substantiate
their findings.

SOCIAL-PROBLEMS ORIENTATION

Those who first began to study the migrants from Appalachia took a strong
social-problems orientation (Leybourne, 1937; Caldwell, 1940; Killian, 1953;
Giffin, 1956; Henderson, 1966; Montgomery, 1968; Gitlin and Hollander, 1970;
Leeds, 1971). Many of these studies included Appalachian migrants in studies of
poor whites or southern white migrants, without identifying Appalachians
specifically. Morris Caldwell (1940), in one of the first studies of Appalachian
migrants, developed an index of social maladjustment consisting of family,
economic, health, educational, religious, court, and institutional experiences.
He concluded that Appalachian migrants experienced over three times as many
social maladjustments in the city of Lexington, Kentucky, than they experienced in Appalachia. They experienced one and a half times as many problems
as did migrants to Lexington from the Bluegrass area of the state. His conclusions
are echoed by the other writers in their descriptions of broken families, poverty,
unemployment, crime, disaffiliation, and illness.

The most common explanation offered for the maladjustments of Appalachian migrants was the conflict between their culture and the culture which was
dominant in the areas to which they migrated. Roscoe Giffin (1956), for
example, cites the extended kinship system of Appalachians as responsible for

voluntary segregation in Appalachian ghettos. Such a family system often produced overcrowding as relatives moved in with other migrants. The reliance upon kin, and not formal organizations, to meet needs in Appalachian communities meant that Appalachians developed few leadership skills or abilities to work with others in groups. The religious fundamentalism of Appalachians made urban churches, with their emphasis upon social gospel, unattractive. Children frequently dropped out of school because they were not encouraged to stay by parents, relatives, and neighbors, who had little education themselves and regarded education as unimportant. The reluctance to use available health care facilities was due to an acceptance of illness as unavoidable. George Henderson (1966, p. 114) summed up the feelings of many, in concluding that "the cultural conditioning of the southern white immigrant seems to make him less prepared to adjust to urban living than the southern Negro immigrant."

The social-problem orientation, with its emphasis upon cultural conflict, probably remains the dominant perspective in the study of Appalachian migrants. (See, for example, Steve Weiland's introduction to *Perspectives on Urban Appalachians*, 1978, or the special issue of *Mountain Life and Work*, in 1976, devoted to urban Appalachians.) Still, there is reason to be hesitant in accepting that viewpoint. First, the conclusions reached in these studies were almost inevitable, given the procedures used. None of these studies used a representative sample of Appalachian migrants. Most often, these researchers have gone into lower-class slums, described the conditions of the people living there, and attributed their plight to the conflict between their culture and the culture common to urban life. There is nothing to indicate the relative frequency with which Appalachian migrants find themselves living in urban slums, and no attempt is made to explain why cultural conflict prohibits the success of some migrants but not others. Second, these studies frequently are limited to recent migrants from Appalachia. Studies of foreign immigrants to urban areas have generally shown that, after an initial period of adjustment, new migrants obtain parity with other groups. The children of immigrants are likely to do better than their parents. The study of recent migrants and the conclusion that cultural conflict prohibited their success may have been premature. Finally, many of these studies have been conducted by social workers or political activists who stand to gain from the problems of Appalachian migrants. While they have probably not intentionally misrepresented the facts, and may even be accurate, their vested interest makes it difficult to rely upon their conclusions.

ASSIMILATION ORIENTATION

The most notable exception to the social-problems orientation has been the work of James S. Brown, his colleagues, and students. Brown began his work in Appalachian studies with an anthropological account of the social organization of a rural community in Kentucky (Brown, 1950). In 1961, Brown, along with Harry Schwarzweller and Joseph Mangalam, interviewed 161 people who had migrated from Beech Creek since the time of Brown's 1942 study. Most (63 percent) had migrated to southwestern Ohio, and the remainder (35 percent) to other parts of Ohio, Indiana, and central Kentucky. The conclusions reached by Brown and his associates differ from those of the social-problems orientation in three fundamental ways.

First, the kinship structure of Appalachian families is seen as assisting, rather than inhibiting, the adjustment of migrants to urban life. They believe that in many ways the migration system of Appalachians resembles Frederic LePlay's model of stem-family migration. While LePlay stressed the importance of the stem-family in the migration process, Brown and his colleagues analyze the importance of the branch-family. The branch-family (those who have migrated) are able to provide an informational system to potential migrants about the availability of jobs (Brown, Schwarzweller, and Mangalam, 1963; Brown, 1968; Schwarzweller, 1981). When jobs are available, potential migrants are told to come, and when jobs are not available, those same people are told to stay where they are. There is even some indication that industries in the urban North have made use of this system and explicitly told Appalachians they employed about the coming availability of new jobs (Schwarzweller, 1981). As a result of this system, Appalachians migrate only in good economic times and do not add to the burden upon the social welfare system of northern cities. The kinship system further assists the migration process by providing havens for new migrants. Previous migrants provide temporary housing, assistance in locating more permanent housing as well as jobs, and perform as teachers in the socialization of new migrants (Brown, Schwarzweller, and Mangalam, 1963; Brown, 1968). Frequently, potential migrants come to urban areas to visit relatives, and stay only after finding such experiences enjoyable (Schwarzweller, 1981). The branch-family provides not only a tangible assistance to new migrants, but also acts as a social psychological cushion. Schwarzweller and Seggar (1967) found that among new migrants, the greater the degree of involvement with relatives in the area of destination, the greater the migrants' social psychological adjustment in terms of greater identification with the urban locality, less nostalgia, less anomie, greater happiness, less work, and less anxiety. In time, migrants appear to become weaned from this support system and maintain themselves economically, socially, and psychologically without assistance from relatives.

Second, in the assimilation orientation, the socioeconomic attainments of Appalachian migrants are described in positive, instead of negative, terms. According to Schwarzweller (1981), the typical Appalachian migrant finds employment in the factories of the urban North. Although most begin work in unskilled jobs, the majority experience some upward mobility, such that within ten years, less than 20 percent remain at unskilled levels (Crowe, 1964). Larry Morgan analyzed the economic benefits of migration to a sample of eastern Kentucky Appalachians who migrated to either Lexington, Kentucky, or

Cincinnati (Morgan, 1981). He found that family incomes of migrants increased by 41 percent between their last year in eastern Kentucky and their first year in the cities. After migration, their incomes continued to increase, although at slower rates. In a study of West Virginia migrants to Cleveland, John D. Photiadis compared two samples of migrants (one living in a ghetto area and one in the suburbs) to people living in West Virginia (Photiadis, 1970). He found that migrants initially settled in the inner-city ghettos of Cleveland. As they obtained improved occupational skills and an understanding of urban life, they moved to the more affluent suburbs. Both migrants living in the inner city and those living in suburbs were better off than people continuing to live in West Virginia. The key factor which influenced the socioeconomic achievements of Appalachian migrants was their socioeconomic origins (Schwarzweller and Brown, 1967). The greater the social class origins of the migrants, the greater their occupational achievements and standards of living in areas of destination. This relationship was due, in large part, to the higher educational attainments among migrants with higher socioeconomic origins.

Third, the conflict between Appalachian culture and the culture of the larger society is minimized by Schwarzweller and Brown (1969). Several factors contribute to the disappearance of this conflict. The education system, which is universal in Appalachia as well as the rest of the nation, teaches normative patterns of urban America to Appalachian children; they are taught by middle-class-oriented teachers trained in colleges which emphasize urban norms. While the things children learn may not be completely appreciated, Appalachian parents recognize the necessity of education as the means to upward mobility for their children. Second, the mass media bring exposure to urban ways into the homes of Appalachia. REA provided electricity many years ago, and television antennas are as much a part of Appalachian homes as they are of homes in other areas. Finally, Appalachia is economically tied to the rest of the nation. Frozen foods are found in its groceries, copies of New York fashions appear on the clothing racks of eastern Kentucky as soon as they appear in Cincinnati, and McDonalds is as much a part of Appalachian culture as it is of any other. By now, the culture of Appalachia is highly similar to that found in other parts of the nation.

In general, the data available to Brown and his associates have advantages over those used by persons favoring the social-problems approach. They have either taken a sample of migrants and described their attainments after migration or used samples of migrants in both inner cities and suburbs. As a result, they are not restricted to people who have achieved little success and/or who are forced to live in decaying ghettos.

The data which Brown and his associates used still have limitations which restrict their conclusions. First, the migrants from Beech Creek came from a farming area. These people may have had choices which were not available to Appalachians in the mining regions. While the farms could not provide a livelihood for everyone raised there, it was possible for many to stay permanently and for yet others to return temporarily. It was possible for people from Beech Creek to migrate by choice and to depend upon relatives back home until they were established. People in the mining areas left because the mines closed and few who remained behind were capable of providing support. Second, for the most part, the studies of Brown and his associates are limited to recent migrants, as was true of those who took a social-problems orientation. At the same time, their data indicate that the longer migrants have been in the area of destination, the higher their economic achievements have been. There is little to indicate the success of those who migrated some time ago, and nothing is known about the success of their children. Finally, it is difficult to make conclusions about the success of Appalachian migrants without having some knowledge of the success of other groups. Neither Brown and his associates nor those who favor the social-problems approach provide comparisons with migrants from other places or with people who are native to those urban areas.

Only recently have studies begun to provide comparisons between Appalachians and other groups, but these studies are only a beginning. Maloney (1974) and McKee and Obermiller (1978) compare census tracts where Appalachians are believed to live to other census tracts, but neither have data on actual individuals. Hamilton (1970), Peterson et al. (1977) and Philliber (1981) compare Appalachians to other persons, but those studies are restricted to samples from inner-city ghettos. Perhaps the best comparative study to date is Fowler's (see Appalachian Regional Commission, 1979b) analysis of the earnings of recent Appalachian migrants, but his analysis is limited to earnings and his sample to recent migrants. Many questions therefore remain about the experiences of Appalachians who migrated to other places.

Why Did the Appalachians Migrate?

The dominant opinion seems to be that Appalachians migrated in search of better jobs, but there are those who believe that higher welfare benefits drew Appalachians to midwestern cities. For example, Larry Long (1974) explains the higher percentage of welfare recipients among white southern migrants in five cities as the result of the southern Appalachian people's search for improved welfare benefits. Those who have studied the migrants more often conclude that work, not welfare, was the draw (Hamilton, 1970; Photiadis, 1965; Schwarz-weller, 1981). Even those who favor the social-problems orientation conclude that few Appalachian migrants make use of public assistance (Peterson et al., 1977). Welfare was avoided either by staying in Appalachia or by returning there when employment ended (Schwarzweller, 1981).

A close review of existing literature indicates that little information actually exists about the use Appalachian migrants make of welfare. While early migrants may have avoided social services, things may have changed. The urbanization of Appalachians may have made them aware that welfare provides alternatives to returning to Appalachia. They may receive unemployment compensation and use the time to look for work, instead of returning to Appalachia and waiting until they hear of new work. It is possible that some of these people may give up their search and accept welfare benefits as their primary source of income. Welfare benefits have been extended to larger numbers of people, including those who have jobs. Food stamps, for example, provide assistance to low-income families who thus obtain better diets than would otherwise be available. Finally, ties with Appalachia diminish over time. As parents die and old homes are sold, Appalachian migrants and their children lose the alternative of returning. Welfare could become the only choice. How frequent, and under what conditions Appalachian migrants use social services, are unanswered questions.

Where Did the Appalachians Settle?

There are at present three different opinions about the settlement patterns of Appalachian migrants. The oldest opinion, and the one most often described in popular journalism, is that Appalachians have settled in the low-income ghettos frequently found in the inner cities of midwestern metropolitan areas. There a cycle of poverty soon traps the migrants and their children, denying them an opportunity to move to other areas. Gary Fowler (1981) analyzed data from the public school enrollments of Cincinnati. He found that Appalachians were most often found in white, low-income areas, near the central city. As distance increased from the central city and as incomes of the area increased, the proportion of Appalachians decreased.

John D. Photiadis (1970) holds to a two-stage settlement pattern in which migrants originally settle in low-income, inner-city neighborhoods but then migrate to higher-income suburban areas as their economic situations improve. The West Virginia migrants he describes first migrated to one of the Appalachian ghettos of Cleveland. Frequent contact with relatives and friends who had also moved from West Virginia provided a cushion during the transition to urban life. As these people obtained better jobs and built up some savings, the majority moved to suburban areas where they were able to live in homes they had purchased.

Brown and his associates (Schwarzweller, Brown, and Mangalam, 1971) argue that many migrants never experience ghetto life. Instead, the migration patterns of Appalachians are determined by their socioeconomic status at the time of migration. Those who come from unskilled, low-income families settle in urban ghettos, but those who come from semi-skilled, skilled, and white-collar, higher-income families do not. In both instances, migrants settle near friends and relatives.

The conflicts in these perspectives could have emerged from studies of people at different stages of the migration process, instead of from any real differences in their findings. Most studies of Appalachian migrants have been limited to people who recently moved from Appalachia. The conclusion that they are caught in a cycle of poverty may have been prematurely based upon observations of people who, given a little time, will move upward, both economically and residentially. Those persons who first left Appalachia were of higher socioeconomic status (Schwarzweller and Seggar, 1967) than more recent migrants. It may be that they were able to acquire good jobs and buy homes in suburban areas, as Photiadis describes, but it may not be possible for new migrants to repeat their experience. It is also possible that these migrants of higher socioeconomic origins help their relatives to settle in homes near them, but the majority of migrants who come from lower socioeconomic families may continue to settle in Appalachian ghettos where they become trapped. Existing data neither adequately document the distribution of Appalachians within urban areas, nor permit conclusions about the effects of time and other factors upon their settlement patterns.

What Have Been the Attainments of Appalachian Migrants?

Appalachians have been described as a drain upon the social welfare systems of cities which have received them (e.g., Long, 1974); as poor people unable to find work, forced to live in decaying ghettos, but too proud for welfare (e.g., Henderson, 1966); or as a major source of industrial workers in urban factories (e.g., Schwarzweller, 1981). It is possible to find examples of each of these, but it is difficult to make generalizations from examples. Only representative samples can provide the data necessary for conclusions about the attainments of Appalachians who moved to the cities.

There is reasonably good evidence that those people who left Appalachia obtained better-paying jobs in urban areas than they previously held (Hamilton, 1970; Appalachian Regional Commission, 1979b; Morgan, 1981) and hold jobs better than those held by people remaining in Appalachia (Hamilton, 1970; Photiadis, 1970). However, the attainments of Appalachians may be below those of migrants from other areas and of people who are natives of the cities which received them (Appalachian Regional Commission, 1979b). Appalachia is an economically depressed region. The economic standard of living is frequently so low that it would be difficult to move away and not do better. Despite the improvement Appalachians experienced, it would still be possible for them to occupy the bottom rung of the urban socioeconomic ladder.

The attainments of the children of Appalachian migrants are an essential link in determining the prospects for those people. Many foreign immigrants to American cities did not obtain a great deal of economic success themselves. Poor educational backgrounds and an unfamiliarity with urban customs were disadvantages which could not be immediately overcome. However, the children of these immigrant groups did obtain economic parity with those whose parents were natives (Blau and Duncan, 1967). The great migration from Appalachia began almost 40 years ago. By now, the children of those first migrants have completed their educations and taken their places in the labor force. It is their attainments, more so than the attainments of their parents, which are the critical gauge of the economic success of Appalachians in urban areas.

To What Extent Have Appalachians Become Integrated into the Social and Political Systems of Urban Areas?

Most scholars and journalists who have studied Appalachian migrants have come to the conclusion that Appalachians have taken up residence in the cities without becoming a part of those communities. The usual explanation is that Appalachian culture is not conducive to integration with urban life. Their close family ties cause them to cluster in ghettos where they have minimal contact with non-Appalachians (Giffin, 1956). With their stress on independence, they seek their own solutions to problems, instead of working with others or joining organizations (Giffin, 1956). The fundamentalism of their religion causes them to reject established churches found in cities which stress a more social form of religion (Weller, 1966). Their failure to recognize the importance of education leads to a high dropout rate in school (Henderson, 1966; Wagner, 1975). They frequently travel to Appalachia for visits with relatives, instead of developing relationships in their new communities. At best they are seen as nostalgic for life as it was back home and planning to return the first chance they get (Killian, 1953; Fowler, 1978).

Despite the almost universal conclusion that Appalachians have not integrated into the social and political life of the areas to which they migrated, few attempts have been made to document that lack. Even the case studies which describe poverty among Appalachians living in ghettos do not include much about the interaction with churches, schools, urban bureaucracies, social groups, or political behavior. The implication seems to be that since no such descriptions exist, the social and political integration must be absent. It could, however, be possible that insufficient attempts have been made to study the integration of Appalachians into urban areas.

What Is the Effect of Appalachian Cultural Values and Involvement in Appalachian Kinship Systems upon the Economic, Social, and Political Achievements of Appalachian Migrants?

Reference to the importance of Appalachian culture in understanding the experiences of Appalachian migrants is found throughout the literature. The recent *Perspectives on Urban Appalachians* (1978) includes selections on the impact that Appalachian culture has on racial prejudice (Killian, 1953), social welfare practice (Maloney, 1978), education (Wagner, 1978), health practices (Watkins, 1978), employment (Powles, 1964), and involvement with the legal system (Huelsman, 1969). While not all agree that Appalachian culture produces conflict for migrants in urban areas (Jones, 1976; Fisher, 1977; Fowler, 1978), it does appear to be the opinion of the majority.

Studies of the extent of Appalachian cultural values, or of the impact which those values have upon outcomes for Appalachian migrants, are almost nonexistent. Schwarzweller and Seggar (1967) studied the effect that involvement within an Appalachian kinship network had for adjustment to urban areas, and came to the conclusion that those who had the greatest involvement with kin made the best adjustment. This is contradictory to the expectations set forth by most advocates of the importance of Appalachian values. For most, Appalachian cultural values are accepted by faith as the chief factor responsible for the experiences of Appalachians in urban areas. Neither the extent nor the importance of those values has been empirically demonstrated.

How Have the Experiences of Appalachians in Urban Areas Affected Their Mental Health and Outlook on Life?

Much popular journalism leads to the conclusion that Appalachians are unhappy in urban cities. However, Photiadis's (1970) study of West Virginians in Cleveland and Brown's and his associates' study of Kentuckians in Cincinnati (Schwarzweller and Seggar, 1967) find the social-psychological attitudes of those migrants to be relatively positive. Photiadis's comparison with people living in West Virginia shows that migrants were less alienated than were those remaining in their home state. A majority of migrants living in the suburbs and a majority of migrants living in the inner-city ghettos felt that life was better than it had ever been before. Schwarzweller and Seggar found that the social-psychological attitudes of migrants were especially good among new migrants who maintained an active involvement with other relatives in Cincinnati. This contradicts the expectations of those who lean toward a cultural-conflict interpretation of Appalachians' experiences in urban areas. How representative those findings are has yet to be determined.

To What Extent Have Appalachians Developed as a Subgroup Within the Cities to Which They Migrated?

Perhaps one of the indications of a lack of knowledge about Appalachian migrants is the lack of consensus over whether they should be considered a subgroup within the cities to which they migrated. Phillip Obermiller (1977), who provides a review of the different perspectives on this issue, indicates that the question has broad implications for the people involved. Political pressure by organized subgroups is increasingly brought to bear upon elected officials and administrators of cities. If Appalachians are a subgroup, then their political organization should increase their ability to obtain services from local governments. Special legislation is frequently targeted to meet the needs of subgroups within society. Efforts are made to increase opportunities for those who have been at a disadvantage because of race, religion, or national origin. The discrimination against Appalachians in urban areas could be as great as it has been for any other group, and yet they are denied help because they are not recognized as a subgroup.

In some ways, Appalachian migrants clearly do not form a subgroup in the sense that we think of an ethnic group as a subgroup. They probably have no easily identifiable unique features which would make identification inevitable.

They may be black or white and have surnames which read like the pages out of a telephone directory. Recent migrants may speak with a noticeable accent, but the accent is similar to that found throughout the South and in the small towns and rural areas of the Midwest. Even the cultural values which are stressed as being so important are the values which have always been basic to rural America. Many Appalachians living in urban areas do not identify themselves as part of a subgroup (Miller, 1976). If Appalachians are a subgroup, many potential members, especially those of higher socioeconomic status, choose to pass rather than identify themselves as Appalachians. Finally, if cultural heritage is the basis for recognition of Appalachians as a subgroup, advocates are faced with the dilemma that migrants come from a diversity of backgrounds instead of a single cultural heritage. People in farming areas are different from people in coal-mining regions and people in Appalachian cities are different from those in isolated rural areas. Loyalties which exist are not to Appalachia, but are to local communities from which migrants came.

Despite these reservations, there are indications that Appalachians are a subgroup within urban areas where they migrated. The strongest evidence is that they are frequently recognized and treated as a subgroup by others who live in those cities. McCoy and Watkins (1981) have collected jokes told about Appalachians in midwestern cities. They demonstrate that the same jokes which reflect negative stereotypes of blacks and other groups in some cities are told about Appalachians in midwestern cities. These jokes are accompanied by other indications that people in midwestern cities have formed negative impressions about Appalachian migrants. There is also reason to believe that Appalachian migrants in a particular city may share a common cultural heritage. Migrants in a particular city come disproportionately from a given section of Appalachia. Their heritage would be more homogeneous than would be true for Appalachia as a whole.

If evidence is found that Appalachian migrants form enclaves within the cities where they settle, make friendships and intermarry with others from Appalachia, organize religious groups more characteristic of Appalachia than of cities, exhibit cultural traits not commonly found in cities, and/or identify themselves as a subgroup, then there will be greater reason to conclude that they have, in fact, become one of the subgroups of American cities.

2

APPALACHIANS IN CINCINNATI

Cincinnati has been one of the major receiving centers for migrants from the Appalachian region. The Urban Appalachian Council estimates that over 100,000 Southern Appalachians have moved to Cincinnati since 1940 (Maloney, 1978). An estimated 75,000 to 80,000 became permanent residents there. The children born to these migrants inflate the number of first- and second-generation Appalachians estimated living in the Cincinnati Metropolitan Area to between 150,000 and 200,000 people (or about 20 percent of the total population).

According to McCoy and Brown (1981), southern Appalachian migrants to Cincinnati have predominantly come from eastern Kentucky. In each of the decades since 1940, over 30 percent came from the coal-mining area of eastern Kentucky and another 17 percent from nearby subsistence farming communities. Fifteen percent of Cincinnati's migrants came from eastern Tennessee. In more recent years, Cincinnati has begun to receive a number of migrants from West Virginia.

Two factors made Cincinnati attractive to potential migrants from Appalachia. First, Cincinnati is the closest major industrial center to areas of eastern Kentucky, eastern Tennessee, and much of West Virginia. It is located in southwestern Ohio, adjacent to the area designated as part of Appalachia by the Appalachian Regional Commission. Major highways and public transportation routes made Cincinnati an easy destination by either car or bus. Second, the economy of Cincinnati is based upon a widely diversified industrial structure. It is the world's leading manufacturer of machine parts and soap products. In addition, automobile assembly plants, building-products firms, and a major division of General Electric are located there. Several smaller industries also

12

have manufacturing plants there. These factories provided potential employment to migrants coming from rural backgrounds with limited educations.

In 1975 the Cincinnati Area Project surveyed the relative experiences of Appalachians living in the Cincinnati Metropolitan Area. The Cincinnati Area Project is a training program used to teach undergraduate students, in the Department of Sociology at the University of Cincinnati, basics in survey research. Students from that program, complemented by a team of professional interviewers, collected the necessary data.

They conducted 595 interviews with adults living in Hamilton County, Ohio. Hamilton County includes all of Cincinnati and many of the major suburbs. In 1970 it had a population of 923,000 people, which was 68 percent of the total metropolitan-area population. The counties within the metropolitan area not included in the survey are located in northern Kentucky (outside the Appalachian region), southwestern Ohio (including Clermont County, which is part of the Appalachian region), and Indiana. The exclusion of northern Kentucky presents the greatest problem in the generalization of these data. The northern Kentucky counties of the Cincinnati Metropolitan Area probably receive a large number of migrants from Appalachia. While no differences are expected between migrants in the two areas, the elimination of northern Kentucky may produce an underestimation of the numbers of Appalachians in the metropolitan area.

Participants in the survey were selected through the use of a multistage probability sample with quotas used at the final stage (Sudman, 1966). A random sample of 119 blocks was selected, with the probability of a block's selection being proportional to the number of households there. Interviewers were assigned a random starting point on each block and instructed to proceed in a clockwise direction around the block and conduct interviews until quotas were complete. Five interviews were collected from each block, with quotas assigned based upon the distribution of the population at the time of the 1970 census. The distribution of the population was based upon sex, age of males (under 30; 30 to 59; 60 and over), and employment of females (working or not working). These characteristics were chosen because they are the factors which contribute most to low response rates in simple random samples (Sudman, 1966). This sampling procedure has previously been shown to produce representative samples, with standard errors approximately the same as those found in simple random samples (Sudman, 1966).

There is no consensus on the exact boundaries of the Appalachian region. Since the people have not been recognized as an important group to study (and until recently, qualified for no special government programs), there was no reason to set definite boundaries to the region. John C. Campbell (1921), in the first major study of Appalachia, included 256 counties in nine states. He used the boundaries of the Mason-Dixon Line on the north, the Blue Ridge Mountains on the east, and the Allegheny-Cumberland Plateau on the west to form a rough triangle defined by physical characteristics of the geography.

Thomas R. Ford (1962), in the second major study of Appalachia, limited the area to 190 counties in seven states, eliminating western Maryland and north-western South Carolina entirely. The two definitions cover approximately the same area, but Ford limits his study to state economic areas which are entirely within the Appalachian region. State economic areas are counties grouped by the Bureau of the Census because they have a similar economic base. Data available for state economic areas cannot be obtained about individual counties from the Bureau of the Census. Consequently, Ford used a definition of Appalachia for which data were available. Finally, in 1965 the Appalachian Regional Commission was created to direct federal funding for the economic development of the region. The legislation which was enacted defined Appalachia as including 397 counties located in 13 states. Portions of Ohio, Pennsylvania, New York, and Mississippi, which had never before been included in definitions of Appalachia, were included as part of the region. While the commission's definition encompassed all of the area previously thought of as Appalachia, it was expanded to obtain necessary political support. In the Cincinnati Area Project, the Appalachian Regional Commission's definition was used to set the boundaries of Appalachia, with the exclusion of Clermont County, Ohio. Clermont County is part of the Standard Metropolitan Area of Cincinnati, and people whose origins are there are considered native to the Cincinnati area.

In the Cincinnati Area Project survey, 165 persons (or 28 percent of those surveyed) were either born in the Appalachian region or had at least one parent from the region. Table 2.1 shows the race, sex, age, and generational composition of those people. The majority (84 percent) are white. This is to be

TABLE 2.1
Race, Sex, Age, and Generation of Appalachians in Cincinnati

Variable	Percent	Number
Race		
Black	16	27
White	84	138
Sex (whites only)		
Male	44	60
Female	56	78
Age (whites only)		
Less than 30	30	41
30-44	29	40
45-59	22	30
60 and older	20	27
Generation (whites only)		
First	59	80
Second	41	56

expected since the Appalachian region itself is predominantly white: According to the Appalachian Regional Commission (1977), 93 percent of the population of the region was white in 1970. While a higher proportion of blacks are found among Appalachians in Cincinnati than are living in the region, Appalachia lacked a sufficient pool of potential black migrants to produce a sizable percentage in cities where they located.

It is essential to recognize that Appalachians may be an important subgroup among blacks as well as whites. Those factors which contribute to the experiences of white Appalachian migrants may be equally important to those blacks who are Appalachian (*Mountain Life and Work*, 1976). Unfortunately, this study does not have enough blacks to analyze the experiences of those who are Appalachians. For that reason, the 27 blacks who are Appalachian are grouped with other blacks into a single category in these analyses and not included as Appalachians.

Of the white Appalachians in this survey, 59 percent were first-generation migrants. That is, they were born in one of the counties of Appalachia. The other 41 percent had been born outside Appalachia but had at least one parent born within the region. Comparisons will be made between the two groups as one means of understanding the adaptations of Appalachians with the passage of time.

Most of the white Appalachians either migrated from Appalachian counties in Kentucky or had parents who came from there (see Table 2.2): 56 percent of the first-generation migrants were born in Kentucky; 47 percent of the fathers and 40 percent of the mothers of second-generation migrants also were Kentuckians. No other state approached Kentucky as a sending area for Appalachians in Cincinnati, including the Appalachian counties of Ohio. Few of the migrants came from northern Appalachia to Cincinnati, and most of those who did were from Ohio. Only 16 percent of the first-generation migrants were born in northern Appalachia, with 10 percent of these from Ohio and the remainder from Pennsylvania. Only 8 percent of the fathers of second-generation migrants and 18 percent of the mothers were from northern Appalachia. Even fewer migrants came from the extreme southern sections of Appalachia found in Alabama, Georgia, and Mississippi. Only 4 percent of the first generation Appalachians were born there, and only 4 percent of the fathers and 2 percent of the mothers of second-generation migrants. White Appalachians in Cincinnati migrated almost entirely from that section of Appalachia which is called the Southern Highlands, and the majority of those migrants were from Kentucky.

Many of the second generation Appalachians in Cincinnati had only one parent that was Appalachian. Table 2.3 shows that only 41 percent of the second-generation Appalachians had two parents from Appalachia, while the remainder had only one; 28 percent of the fathers and 31 percent of the mothers were not Appalachian. Most of the fathers who were not Appalachian were also not born in the Cincinnati area (10 percent were from Cincinnati, 18 percent were not), but most of the mothers were Cincinnatians (19 percent from Cincinnati, 12 percent not).

TABLE 2.2
Place of Birth of First-Generation White Appalachian Migrants
and Parents of Second-Generation Migrants
(in percent)

| | | Second Generation | |
Birthplace	First Generation	Father	Mother
Alabama	4	4	2
Georgia	0	0	0
Kentucky	56	47	40
Maryland	0	2	0
Mississippi	0	0	0
New York	0	0	2
North Carolina	0	0	0
Ohio	10	4	10
Pennsylvania	6	4	6
South Carolina	0	0	0
Tennessee	8	2	2
Virginia	6	4	2
West Virginia	10	7	6
Cincinnati Metropolitan Area	–	10	19
Neither Appalachia nor Cincinnati	–	18	12
Number of cases	80	57	52

TABLE 2.3
Origins of Second-Generation White Appalachians in Cincinnati

Origin	Percent
Place of birth	
Cincinnati Metropolitan Area	71
Outside Appalachia but not in Cincinnati	29
Origins of Parents	
Both Appalachian	41
Only father Appalachian	31
Only mother Appalachian	28
Number of cases	56

A number of the second-generation Appalachians in Cincinnati were born outside Appalachia and outside Cincinnati. Their parents moved from Appalachia to somewhere other than Cincinnati, and the children moved to Cincinnati. These people are first-generation migrants from some place other than Appalachia, but they are also second-generation migrants from Appalachia. While they are treated in this study as second-generation Appalachian migrants, their backgrounds are perhaps influenced by both their Appalachian heritage and by the place where their parents located.

As a result of marital and migration patterns, several different types of people are classified as second-generation Appalachians. There are people who have both parents from Appalachia and there are those who have only one. Those who have one parent who is Appalachian may have a second parent from Cincinnati or from someplace else. The parent who is not Appalachian may be the mother or the father. Parents who are Appalachian may have migrated to Cincinnati, or they may have moved to some other place and the child then moved to Cincinnati. Any effect which migration from Appalachia has upon people should be reduced in the second generation, not only because the second generation was born outside Appalachia, but also because they most often have only one parent from Appalachia. Assimilation into Cincinnati may be delayed, however, either because the non-Appalachian parent was not from Cincinnati or because the second-generation migrant from Appalachia was born outside Cincinnati. It would be useful to put these different types of people into separate groups, for clearly they are not a singular category. Unfortunately, the too-few cases in this analysis make that separation impossible.

Appalachians in this study have been living in Cincinnati for many years. Although the 1960s produced the largest migration (30 percent), 64 percent of the first-generation migrants were there before that time (see Table 2.4); and 21 percent of these migrants came to Cincinnati prior to 1940, during the years of the great depression or before. On the average, first-generation migrants have been living in Cincinnati for 24 years. Only 5 percent of the first-generation migrants in this study have moved to Cincinnati since 1970. This migration pattern is similar to that shown by McCoy and Brown (1981), which shows a large migration out of Appalachia from the end of World War II through the 1960s, with few migrants leaving Appalachia after that time. These data demonstrate, though, that the migration to Cincinnati from Appalachia goes back to before World War II. There may be important differences between migrants who have been in Cincinnati for many years and those who have come more recently.

Most of the first-generation migrants moved to Cincinnati while they were young — 30 percent of the migrants were 15 or younger. Most of these people probably moved with their parents to Cincinnati. Another 42 percent moved to Cincinnati between the ages of 16 and 25, at a time when they were probably looking for their first jobs and starting a family. Few migrants came to Cincinnati after they were 25. There are a few people (8 percent) who moved to Cincinnati after they reached 50. Unlike those who came in search of work,

TABLE 2.4
Age at Migration and Year of Migration among First-Generation White Appalachian Migrants

Variable	Percent
Age at migration	
0 to 15	30
16 to 20	29
21 to 25	13
26 to 30	9
31 to 49	11
50 and older	8
Number of cases	78
Median age	20
Mean age	21
Year of migration	
Prior to 1940	21
1940 to 1949	21
1950 to 1959	22
1960 to 1969	30
1970 to 1975	5
Number of cases	80
Median years in Cincinnati	22
Mean years in Cincinnati	24

these older people may have moved to Cincinnati to be closer to their children.

Many of the second-generation migrants in Cincinnati have also lived there for many years. They have in fact lived there an average of 33 years, and have an average age of 38, compared to an average age of 46 among first-generation migrants. While first-generation migrants are older, the ages of the two groups are close enough to make comparisons between the two groups fruitful.

Throughout this study, white Appalachians are compared to three other groups. First, white Appalachians are compared to whites who have been native to the Cincinnati area for three or more generations. Appalachian migrants have previously been compared to nonmigrants in Appalachia (Photiadis, 1970) and to themselves before migration (Morgan, 1981). People back home and oneself at an earlier time are important reference groups for evaluating success, particularly in the first years after migration takes place. Over time, these groups probably become less important and comparisons begin to be made with others in the immediate environment. Migrants may experience success, compared to those who have stayed behind, but continue at a disadvantage compared to people who are already in the area to which they migrated. Second, white Appalachians are compared to whites who migrated to the Cincinnati area from places outside Appalachia. If the experiences of Appalachians are the same as these people's, then migration itself may be an important factor, although an Appalachian heritage is not. If their experiences are different, then it will be possible to separate out the effects of migration and the effects of an Appalachian heritage. Third, white Appalachians are compared to blacks. Much is already known about the disadvantages which blacks experience in Cincinnati and other places. If Appalachians experience less success than other whites in Cincinnati, comparisons with blacks will help to evaluate the significance of that disadvantage.

3

MAKING IT IN THE CITY

NEIGHBORHOOD PATTERNS

The low-income ghettos of Cincinnati have been described as "gateways" where Appalachians first settle, until they are able to move to better areas of the city, or as "catch-basins" where migrants become trapped by poverty (Adams, 1971; Maloney, 1974). Despite that characterization, the majority of first- and second-generation Appalachians who participated in this study have never lived in a low-income neighborhood. They have always lived in the stable working-class or middle-income areas of the city and its suburbs.

The 1970 median income of neighborhoods was used to measure the type of neighborhood in which people had lived in the past or were living presently. Maloney (1974, p. 13) found a high correlation (.796) existed between median family income and a more general measure of socioeconomic status. Neighborhoods were grouped into four quartiles with approximately equal numbers of participants living in each area at present.

Many Appalachians did originally live in the lowest-income neighborhoods when they first moved to the Cincinnati area, or their parents were living there when they were born. Table 3.1 shows that 40 percent of the Appalachians originally lived in one of these neighborhoods. An additional 38 percent lived within the second quartile, making a total of 78 percent of the Appalachians who originally lived in the poorer half. This is significantly higher than the percentage of migrants from other areas who first settled in one of those neighborhoods (54 percent), slightly higher than the percentage of natives in the area (64 percent), and significantly lower than the percentage of blacks (86 percent).

TABLE 3.1
First Neighborhoods of White Appalachians, White Migrants from Other Areas, Blacks, and White Natives in Cincinnati
(in percent)

Variable	White Appalachian Migrants	Other White Migrants	Blacks	White Natives
Median income of neighborhood				
Less than $9,000	40	32*	70*	35
$ 9,000 to $10,999	38	22	16	31
$11,000 to $12,999	10	28	12	23
$13,000 and above	12	19	3	11
Number of cases	128	190	96	128
Median median income of neighborhood[a]	$9,317	$10,143	$6,556	$9,655
Location of neighborhood				
Inner city	60	58	85*	65
Suburb	40	42	15	35
Number of cases	133	199	98	136
Reason for living in neighborhood				
Job related	39	29	12	21*
Family related	30	30	44	46
Housing related	26	29	38	25
School related	4	12	1	5
Other	1	0	5	2
Number of cases	112	164	78	99

*Significantly different from percentages for white Appalachian migrants (p < .05).

[a]This means that 50 percent of the people in each group live in a neighborhood with a median family income greater than the value indicated. Significance can not be calculated.

Comparisons of the median income of neighborhoods make it easier to see the relative standings of the neighborhoods in which the different groups first lived in Cincinnati. White migrants from places other than Appalachia initially settled in the best neighborhoods: 50 percent of them settled in neighborhoods which had a median income of more than $10,143, whereas 50 percent of the Appalachians first settled in neighborhoods with median incomes of more than $9,317, which is about the same as the figure for Cincinnati natives ($9,655).

Blacks settled in distinctly poorer neighborhoods, 50 percent of them settling in neighborhoods with median incomes of less than $6,556.

The majority of Appalachians did initially settle within the city limits of Cincinnati instead of the suburbs: 60 percent of the Appalachians were either born within the inner city or moved there when they first came to Cincinnati. This percentage is about the same as that for white migrants from other areas (58 percent) and for whites who are native to the area (65 percent). Only the blacks settled within the inner city more frequently than Appalachians.

The largest difference between Appalachians and other groups comes in the comparisons of why they (or their parents) chose to first settle in the neighborhoods they did. Appalachians most frequently chose to live where they did because of job-related reasons, usually closeness to work. Almost 40 percent of Appalachians cited this as the most important factor in choosing the first neighborhood where they lived. With all the emphasis on the importance of the Appalachian family, both white natives of Cincinnati and blacks more frequently cited family factors in their choice of neighborhood, and white migrants from other areas cited the family as often as did Appalachians. In at least this instance, the family is not a more important factor to Appalachians than it is to other groups. Schools were an important consideration only to white migrants from other areas, and to only 12 percent of them. The quality of housing was cited by about a quarter of the three white groups and by 38 percent of the blacks.

During the time they have lived in the Cincinnati area, Appalachians, as well as other groups, have experienced substantial upward mobility to higher-income neighborhoods, often to the suburbs. At the time of the interview, fewer people in all groups were living in low-income neighborhoods and higher percentages were in upper middle-income neighborhoods. Only 22 percent of the first- and second-generation white Appalachians were living in neighborhoods with a median family income of less than $9,000, while 58 percent were now in middle-income areas and 20 percent had moved to the upper-income neighborhoods. While the majority continue to live in the working-class or middle-income areas, there has been a notable decline in white Appalachians living in low-income ghettos and an increased representation in the more affluent sectors. In fact, 50 percent of them now live in neighborhoods with a median income of more than $10,414.

The gap between white Appalachians and white migrants who moved to Cincinnati from other areas has increased slightly during the time the two groups have been in the Cincinnati area. By 1975, only 14 percent of the white migrants from other areas were living in low-income ghettos, while 54 percent were in middle-income neighborhoods and 31 percent were in the upper-income quartile. More than half (59 percent) were in neighborhoods with median family incomes of $11,000 or more, compared to only 38 percent of the Appalachian families. Although white Appalachians have experienced mobility to better-income neighborhoods during the time they have been in the Cincinnati area, their mobility has been less than that experienced by white migrants from other areas. The differences between their median neighborhood incomes increased from $826 in the first neighborhood to a $2,181 advantage in their present neighborhood.

Whites who have been living in the Cincinnati area for three or more generations have experienced about the same amount of mobility to higher-income neighborhoods as have the Appalachians. As a result, the neighborhoods where Appalachians live continue to be similar to those of Cincinnati natives.

TABLE 3.2
Present Neighborhoods of White Appalachians, White Migrants from Other Areas, Blacks, and White Natives in Cincinnati
(in percent)

Variable	White Appalachian Migrants	Other White Migrants	Blacks	White Natives
Median Income of neighborhood				
Less than $9,000	22	14*	56*	15
$ 9,000 to $10,999	40	26	25	34
$11,000 to $12,999	18	28	12	30
$13,000 and above	20	31	7	20
Number of cases	138	201	103	137
Median median income of neighborhood	$10,414	$12,595	$8,143	$11,040
Location of neighborhood				
Inner city	36	39	84*	48*
Suburb	64	61	16	52
Number of cases	138	201	103	137
Reason for living in neighborhood				
Job related	22	13	7*	12
Family related	17	15	18	27
Housing related	54	59	69	51
School related	7	13	5	10
Other	0	0	1	1
Number of cases	128	190	96	128

*Significantly different from percentages for white Appalachian migrants (p < .05).

Blacks have experienced the greatest amount of mobility from low-income neighborhoods to better areas, but continue to have the highest percentages living in low-income neighborhoods. At the time of the survey, 56 percent were still living in the low-income ghettos, compared to 70 percent who first lived there. This 56 percent was twice the percentage of Appalachians and four times the percentage of white migrants from other areas or white natives. The mobility which blacks have experienced has largely been confined to a movement from the low-income areas to the lower middle-income neighborhoods. Only 7 percent were living in the upper-income sectors of the Cincinnati area. While blacks have had greater mobility than Appalachians, their advances have not made up for the initial disadvantage.

The major shift in the neighborhoods of Appalachians has been a movement from the inner city to the suburbs. Indeed, 64 percent of the Appalachians were living in the suburbs at the time of the study. That percentage is greater than the percentage for any of the other groups. Although both white migrants to and natives of Cincinnati have also moved to the suburbs, they have not moved there as frequently as have the Appalachians. This location of large percentages of Appalachians in the suburbs is surprising, given the emphasis upon Appalachian ghettos. While there is little here to indicate that Appalachians have obtained great affluence since migrating, there is even less to indicate that they are trapped in the low-income areas within the inner city.

The reasons Appalachians give for choosing to live in the neighborhoods where they presently do are different from the reasons given for living in their first neighborhoods. While job-related reasons were the most frequent ones cited for living in their first neighborhood, the majority of Appalachians live in their present neighborhood because of the quality of housing. Indirectly, this may indicate that job concerns were of primary importance when Appalachians first migrated to the Cincinnati area, and, as they became settled in their jobs, they were able to shift their attention to quality of life. More Appalachians than other groups continue to live where they do because of job concerns, but it is no longer the major reason.

Few Appalachians cite family reasons as the primary factor in choosing to live in their present neighborhoods. Only 17 percent live where they do to be close to other family members. The stereotype that Appalachians attempt to create family enclaves within the cities where they move is not borne out by these data. Either concerns about their jobs or desires for certain types of housing are much more important.

These findings cast serious doubt upon many of the traditional assumptions about the housing patterns of Appalachians. First, there is little here to indicate that Appalachians migrate to inner-city ghettos where they become trapped in a cycle of poverty. Only 40 percent of the Appalachians originally settled in low-income neighborhoods, and about half that number (22 percent) remained there at the time of this study. These percentages are approximately the same as those of whites who have lived in the Cincinnati area for at least three generations and are only slightly larger than the percentages of white migrants who came to Cincinnati from places outside Appalachia. The descriptions of Appalachian ghettos may make for interesting reading, but they do not appear to be representative of the thousands of people who moved from the Appalachian region to the Cincinnati Metropolitan Area. The people from Appalachia are generally living in the middle-income neighborhoods of the Cincinnati area characteristic of working-class people. They have not become affluent during their years in Cincinnati, but they have shared in a part of the American dream.

There are, of course, different ways of looking at numbers. The percentages indicate that it is not accurate to describe white Appalachians as living in low-income ghettos. However, the percentages of Appalachians which are in those ghettos may translate into several thousand people. In this study, 24 percent of the sample were first- or second-generation white Appalachians. As a percentage of Hamilton County's 1970 population of 923,000, this means an estimated 221,520 white Appalachians are living in the county. If 22 percent of this number is living in low-income ghettos, that means 48,734 people. Concern for these people is entirely justified, but their experiences should not be used as the basis for generalizations about the people from Appalachia.

Second, the importance of the Appalachian family is not supported by the housing patterns of this sample. Initially, only about a third of the Appalachians settled in a neighborhood because of their family. By the time of this study, only about half that number continued to live where they did for family reasons. Family was more important to blacks and white natives of Cincinnati and as important to white migrants from other places. Originally, Appalachians were more concerned about jobs and later about quality of housing. The building of family enclaves and the preservation of extended family networks are not borne out in these data.

There is strong evidence of the suburbanization of Appalachians: 40 percent of the first- and second-generation Appalachians in this study originally settled in a suburb of Cincinnati, not within the city limits. An additional 24 percent had moved from the city to the suburbs. As a result, a higher percentage of Appalachians were living in the suburbs at the time of this study than migrants from other places, natives of Cincinnati, or blacks. This finding supports the earlier findings of Schwarzweller et al. (1971), to the effect that many Appalachians move directly to the suburbs when they migrate; and of Photiadis (1975), to the effect that large numbers of Appalachians experience migration in two stages — first to the inner city and then to the suburbs. Corresponding with this shift is a change from concerns about jobs, as the major factor influencing choice of housing, to selections made on the basis of desirability of housing. Appalachians appear to believe that they have achieved a point in their lives where they can choose to live in the type of place they want to live, and that choice is overwhelmingly a home in the suburbs.

OCCUPATIONAL ATTAINMENTS

A number of factors may be responsible for moving from one place to another. Some people move to cities because they offer a more exciting life style, greater opportunity for wealth, or simply a chance for them to be out on their own. Others come because social services are more easily available. But for Appalachian migrants, the almost universal reason for moving to Cincinnati was to get a job. Table 3.3 shows that 80 percent of the white Appalachians who had moved to Cincinnati came there because of job-related reasons. Some of these people were transferred by companies which already employed them; others were coming to begin a job they had accepted; still others were coming to look. Few Appalachians came to Cincinnati for any other reason.

TABLE 3.3
Reasons for Moving to Cincinnati among White Appalachians,
White Migrants from Other Areas, and Blacks
(in percent)

Reason for Moving to Cincinnati	White Appalachians	Other White Migrants	Blacks
Job	80	66*	46*
Family	12	19	27
Available services	1	9	12
City life	5	0	4
Other	2	6	10
Number of cases	93	110	48

*Significantly different from percentages for white Appalachian migrants (p < .05).

Appalachians cited job-related reasons for coming to Cincinnati more frequently than did either white migrants from other areas or black migrants. Only 66 percent of white migrants from outside Appalachia and 46 percent of black migrants came to Cincinnati for job-related reasons. This means that white migrants from outside Appalachia came to Cincinnati for job-related reasons only about three-fourths as often as did white Appalachians, and blacks came to Cincinnati for job-related reasons only about half as often as did white Appalachians. Clearly, white Appalachians, more than any other group, came to Cincinnati in search of work.

Fewer white Appalachians than other migrants moved to Cincinnati for either family-related reasons or because of available services. Only 12 percent of the white Appalachians came because of their family, compared to 19 percent of the other white migrants and 27 percent of the blacks. Only 1 percent came because of available services, compared to 9 percent of the other white migrants and 12 percent of the blacks. This would seem to cast doubt on two of the explanations sometimes listed as reasons for Appalachian migration. First, the importance of the Appalachian family is not borne out by these data. Few Appalachians in total, and fewer Appalachians than other groups, cited family reasons for migrating to Cincinnati. Second, almost no Appalachians came to Cincinnati because of social service benefits. There is just no support for the thesis that higher welfare benefits have drawn Appalachians to Cincinnati.

TABLE 3.4

**Present Occupations of White Appalachians, White Migrants
from Other Areas, White Natives of Cincinnati, and Blacks**
(in percent)

Status/Distribution	White Appalachian Migrants	Other White Migrants	Blacks	White Natives
Present work status				
Employed	94	93	72*	92
Unemployed and looking for work	6	7	28	8
Number of cases	67	121	65	88
Percent disabled	4	5	13*	1
Occupational distribution				
Professional and managerial	19	44*	14	30*
Clerical and sales	12	20	19	31
Skilled crafts	13	18	10	16
Semiskilled operatives	33	8	23	10
Service workers	19	8	22	11
Unskilled laborers	4	3	14	2
Number of cases	84	143	74	97
Mean SEI score	32	50*	30	44*

*Significantly different from percentages or averages for white Appalachian migrants (p < .05).

If Appalachians came to Cincinnati in order to get a job, then it is reasonable to ask how they have done. Table 3.4 shows that at the time of the survey, 94 percent of the white Appalachians in the labor force were employed. This percentage is approximately the same as that of other white migrants and of white natives in Cincinnati and is much higher than the percentage of blacks, among whom only 72 percent of the labor force were employed. Appalachians have thus succeeded in their search for work, as long as success is defined as simply getting a job.

Some people have theorized that Appalachians who could not find work and were therefore forced to accept welfare benefits would claim physical disabilities to legitimize their situation both to themselves and to others. In fact, the data do not support such a thesis. Only 4 percent of the white Appalachians claimed physical disabilities, which is approximately the same as the figure for other white migrants and for white Cincinnati natives and is lower than the incidence of physical disabilities cited among blacks. The dependence on welfare among white Appalachians has yet to be seen, but clearly those who are unable to find work do not list themselves as disabled.

While white Appalachians have succeeded in their attempts to find work, the jobs they have secured are more frequently of lower status than those held by other white migrants to or natives of Cincinnati. The job distribution of white Appalachians is similar to that of blacks — skewed toward the less monetarily rewarding blue-collar jobs. At the time of the survey, 31 percent of the white Appalachians were employed in white-collar jobs, which is about half the percentage for the other white migrants (64 percent) and white natives of Cincinnati (61 percent). Further, 19 percent of the white Appalachians were employed as professionals or managers, while 44 percent of the white migrants from other areas and 30 percent of the Cincinnati natives were so employed. If success is defined as employment in a professional or managerial position, clearly Appalachians are less successful than other white groups.

Among blue-collar employees, white Appalachians are less likely than white migrants from other areas or white natives of Cincinnati to be employed as skilled workers. Only 13 percent of the white Appalachians, but 18 percent of the other white migrants, and 16 percent of the white natives were skilled workers. Not only are white migrants from other areas and white natives in Cincinnati more likely than white Appalachians to be employed in white-collar positions, but those who are employed as blue-collar workers are more likely to occupy the most prestigious and best-paying jobs.

The majority of white Appalachians (52 percent) are employed either as semiskilled operatives (33 percent) or service workers (19 percent). This is consistent with earlier descriptions of Appalachian migrants as factory workers. More of them are employed in those types of positions than in any other type of work.

The distribution of jobs held by white Appalachians is approximately the same as for blacks. Thirty-three percent of blacks are employed in white-collar jobs, although white Appalachians are more often employed as professionals or managers. Both groups are usually employed in the lower-status blue-collar occupations. Among those who are blue-collar workers, white Appalachians more frequently are employed as semiskilled operatives and blacks as unskilled laborers. Neither group is as successful in its job attainments as are white migrants from other places and white natives.

Since many families depend upon the husband to earn a living and/or emphasize his occupation as primary and the wife's as secondary, the husband's occupation is often used as the comparison basis for measures of relative success. Because of those factors and to make comparison with other studies possible, it is useful to look at the occupational distribution of heads of households instead of that of the participants in the study. The head of a household is defined as the husband if the person is married and as the individual if he or she is unmarried. The occupational distributions of these people are presented in Table 3.5.

TABLE 3.5
Occupations of Heads of Households of White Appalachians, White Migrants from Other Areas, White Natives of Cincinnati, and Blacks (in percent)

Status/Distribution	White Appalachian Migrants	Other White Migrants	Blacks	White Natives
Present work status				
Employed	94	95	80*	95
Unemployed and looking for work	6	5	20	5
Number of cases	99	148	70	106
Occupational distribution				
Professional and managerial	22	39*	12*	28*
Clerical and sales	9	20	21	26
Skilled crafts	22	24	9	25
Semiskilled operatives	33	10	26	12
Service workers	11	5	18	7
Unskilled laborers	3	2	14	2
Number of cases	125	178	85	121

*Significantly different from percentages for white Appalachian migrants (p < .05).

The occupational distributions of heads of households are similar to the distribution of the participants themselves: 31 percent of the white Appalachians are white-collar workers, which is approximately half the percentage of other white migrants (59 percent) and of white natives (54 percent), and about the same as that of blacks in the Cincinnati area (33 percent). Among heads of households, a higher percentage of white Appalachians are employed as professionals or managers (22 percent) than is true of the participants. Still, the percentages are below those of other white migrants and white natives.

The percentage of white Appalachians (22 percent) employed as skilled craft workers is about the same as for other white migrants (24 percent) and white natives (25 percent). However, since fewer migrants from other areas and white natives are employed as blue-collar workers, the distribution within blue-collar occupations is different. The majority of migrants from other areas and natives of Cincinnati who are employed as blue-collar workers are employed in skilled trades, but only 32 percent of white Appalachians who are employed as blue-collar workers are employed in skilled crafts.

Almost half of the heads of households of white Appalachian families are employed as semiskilled operatives or service workers (44 percent), with the majority of these (33 percent) employed as semiskilled operatives. More Appalachians are employed as semiskilled operatives than are any other group.

The distribution of jobs held by heads of households of white Appalachian families is approximately the same as that held by blacks: 31 percent of white Appalachians and 33 percent of blacks are white-collar workers, although almost twice as many white Appalachians are professionals or managers. Among blue-collar workers, fewer blacks are in skilled crafts and more are unskilled laborers or service workers.

Whether studied from the perspective of the individuals themselves or from that of the occupational distributions of heads of households, the occupational achievements of white Appalachians are much below those of white migrants from other areas and white natives of the Cincinnati area and approximately the same as for blacks.

It is common today for both the husband and the wife to work outside the home. Dual-worker families have emerged as opportunities for women have expanded, and provide a way to increase family incomes beyond the earning

TABLE 3.6

Dual-Worker Families among White Appalachians, White Migrants from Other Areas, White Natives of Cincinnati, and Blacks
(in percent)

Number of Spouses Working	White Appalachian Migrants	Other White Migrants	Blacks	White Natives
One	69	50*	49*	53*
Both	31	50	51	46
Number of cases	97	133	59	86

*Significantly different from percentages for white Appalachian migrants (p < .05).

power of a single worker. However, among Appalachians in Cincinnati, dual-worker families continue to be the exception. Families in which both the husband and the wife were present and in which at least one was in the labor force (including the unemployed) are shown in Table 3.6, by whether one or both spouses were in the labor force. Among white migrants from places other than Appalachia, blacks, and white natives in Cincinnati, approximately 50 percent of each group consisted of dual-worker families, which is close to present national statistics. But only 31 percent of the white Appalachian families were dual-worker families. It appears that a rather strong norm continues to exist among white Appalachians: that the husband alone is responsible for the provider role. In this instance, Appalachians abide by a norm which is not common in urban areas. As a result, family incomes may be lower than for families with similar occupational attainments, and the wives may be more dependent upon their husbands since they do not acquire labor force experience which would enable them to support themselves.

While the occupational achievements of white Appalachians are not as great as those of other white migrants or white natives in Cincinnati, many Appalachians have experienced upward mobility over the attainments of their fathers. Table 3.7 shows the occupational distribution of the fathers of the participants in this study. Only 18 percent of the fathers of white Appalachians were white-collar workers, compared to 31 percent of the participants. This is an increase of 13 percent over the span of a generation. Many more fathers were employed as unskilled laborers and farmers (23 percent) than the present generation (4 percent). In part this is due to migration from farms to urban areas. At the same time, there has been a decrease in the representation of white Appalachians in skilled trades. While 22 percent of the fathers of white Appalachians were skilled craftsmen, only 13 percent of the present generation are similarly employed. Because skilled trades are frequently unionized and open only through apprenticeships, migrants may find that they are prevented from entering skilled trades found in urban areas because they lack the necessary contacts. In any case, they have been less successful than their fathers in obtaining positions in the better blue-collar jobs. The greatest increase in blue-collar employment has been among service workers. As much as anything, this reflects a change in the availability of such positions. Service workers have increased among all groups as the demand for such occupations has increased. There has been no change in the percentage of Appalachians employed in semiskilled jobs. Overall, the comparison of fathers' occupations with those of the Appalachian participants in this study shows an increase in the average Socioeconomic Index (SEI) score of nine points, from 23 to 32.

White migrants from other areas and blacks have experienced approximately the same degree of upward mobility from the occupations of their fathers as have white Appalachians. The mean SEI score for other white migrants increased by eight points and the mean score for blacks increased by nine. The increased occupational achievements of other white migrants is largely among

TABLE 3.7
Occupations of Fathers of White Appalachians, White Migrants from Other Areas, White Natives of Cincinnati, and Blacks
(in percent)

Occupational Distribution	White Appalachian Migrants	Other White Migrants	Blacks	White Natives
Professional and managerial	13	30*	6*	27*
Clerical and sales	5	12	7	12
Skilled crafts	22	28	26	37
Semiskilled operatives	35	13	13	16
Service workers	3	4	8	5
Unskilled laborers	10	4	17	3
Farmers	13	10	23	1
Number of cases	127	190	87	130
Mean SEI score	23	42*	21	42*

*Significantly different from percentages or averages for white Appalachian migrants (p <.05).

white-collar workers: 42 percent of the fathers were white-collar workers, compared to 64 percent of the present generation. This increase has taken place in both professional/managerial positions and clerical/sales. The greatest decreases have taken place among skilled trades (from 28 percent to 18 percent) and farmers (10 percent). Approximately the same percentages are employed as semiskilled, service, and unskilled workers. Among blacks, there has been a major increase in their representation in white-collar jobs: 33 percent of the present generation are employed as white-collar workers, compared to 13 percent of the fathers. These increases have also been in both professional/ managerial and clerical/sales positions. There has also been a major increase among blacks employed as service workers (from 8 percent to 22 percent) and semiskilled trades (from 13 percent to 23 percent). However, fewer blacks are employed in skilled trades (down from 26 percent to 10 percent). While blacks have increased their representation in white-collar positions, they show decreased proportions in the better blue-collar jobs.

White natives of Cincinnati show the least mobility from the occupational distribution of their fathers. The mean SEI score for the present generation is 44, compared to a score of 42 among fathers. While there has been an increase in white-collar representation, from 39 percent to 61 percent, the increase is almost totally among clerical/sales positions; 27 percent of the fathers and 30 percent of the present generation were employed as professionals or managers.

The greatest decrease has occurred among skilled trades (from 37 percent to 16 percent).

Most white Appalachians began their own careers in Cincinnati. Only 38 percent ever worked before moving to the Cincinnati area. Migrants from other areas had more frequently begun their careers first and subsequently moved to Cincinnati: 68 percent were previously employed. Whether measured by the occupations they held prior to moving or by the first occupations they held in Cincinnati, neither white Appalachians, nor other white migrants, nor white natives in Cincinnati show much change in their occupational distributions. Table 3.8 shows the distributions of the first occupations participants held in Cincinnati. The mean SEI scores for the first occupations are almost identical to the present scores for the three white groups. Blacks show upward mobility during their careers.

TABLE 3.8
First Cincinnati Occupation of White Appalachians, White Migrants from Other Areas, White Natives of Cincinnati, and Blacks
(in percent)

Occupational Distribution	White Appalachian Migrants	Other White Migrants	Blacks	White Natives
Professional and managerial	10	35*	4*	18*
Clerical and sales	26	31	16	44
Skilled crafts	14	12	9	10
Semi-skilled operatives	29	15	20	16
Service workers	14	4	35	8
Unskilled laborers	7	4	15	6
Number of cases	117	163	88	126
Mean SEI Score	31	48*	24*	41*

*Significantly different from percentages or averages for white Appalachian migrants ($p < .05$).

While 31 percent of the Appalachians are presently employed as white-collar workers, 36 percent were originally employed that way. There has been an increase in professionals and managers, from 10 percent to 19 percent, probably because some people have been promoted from lower white-collar posts to management. The distribution among blue-collar occupations is almost the same for first occupations and present occupations in Cincinnati. Other white migrants and white natives in Cincinnati show identical patterns to white Appalachians —

an increase among professionals and managers, a corresponding decrease among clerical/sales workers, and general stability among blue-collar occupations.

Blacks are the only group which show much career mobility. The mean SEI score for present occupations is six points higher than the scores for the first occupations held in Cincinnati. The major increase has come in representation among white-collar workers. The percentage who are professionals and managers increased from 4 percent to 14 percent and the percentage who are clerical and sales workers increased from 16 percent to 19 percent. While few whites appear to have crossed the manual/nonmanual barrier into white-collar employment, many blacks have. This mobility is perhaps the result of recent attempts to upgrade levels of opportunity for blacks in the United States. It should be noted that they still remain disproportionately at the lower ranks of the occupational distribution.

Table 3.9 shows the rates of mobility from the father's occupation to the person's present occupation and to the occupation of the head of household. It also shows career mobility from the first occupation in Cincinnati to the present occupation. Intergenerational mobility rates for white Appalachians are approximately the same as for other white migrants, whether measured by the individual's occupation or the occupation of the head of household. Almost half of those in each group have experienced upward mobility from their fathers' occupations, while about a fourth have been downwardly mobile and the other fourth stable. Intergenerational mobility rates of white Cincinnati natives are slightly lower. Only 38 percent have been upwardly mobile. This corresponds to a more general finding that migrants are more occupationally mobile than nonmigrants. Blacks have experienced the highest degree of intergenerational mobility: 58 percent hold occupations higher than the occupations of their fathers. Opportunities for blacks in the present generation appear to be better than in the past.

Upward intragenerational mobility among white Appalachians is approximately the same among other white migrants and white Cincinnati natives — 23 percent, 22 percent and 21 percent, respectively. Blacks have experienced much greater intragenerational mobility (34 percent) than have these groups. At the same time, downward mobility among white Appalachians is much higher than for any of the other groups (27 percent). In fact, more white Appalachians have experienced downward mobility during their careers than experienced upward mobility. A detailed analysis of the mobility tables shows that this downward mobility is caused by the fact that many white Appalachians leave clerical/sales positions for lower-status blue-collar jobs.

Not only are the average occupational achievements of white Appalachians lower than among other white migrants or white natives of Cincinnati, but fewer Appalachians believe they are qualified for a better job than they presently hold. While 51 percent of the white Appalachians felt they were qualified for a better job, more white migrants from other areas (56 percent) and natives of Cincinnati (58 percent) believed they had qualifications for

TABLE 3.9
**Occupational Mobility of White Appalachians, White Migrants
from Other Areas, White Natives of Cincinnati, and Blacks
(in percent)**

Mobility	White Appalachian Migrants	Other White Migrants	Blacks	White Natives
From father's occupation to present occupation				
Upwardly mobile	44	48	58	38
Downwardly mobile	26	17	29	28
Stable	30	35	13	34
Number of cases	73	133	62	92
From father's occupation to head of household's occupation				
Upwardly mobile	53	45	56*	38
Downwardly mobile	20	22	33	24
Stable	27	33	11	37
Number of cases	114	168	72	115
From first Cincinnati occupation to present occupation				
Upwardly mobile	23	22*	34	21
Downwardly mobile	27	12	14	17
Stable	51	65	51	62
Number of cases	79	136	70	94

*Significantly different from percentages for white Appalachian migrants (p $<$ .05).

better jobs. Blacks far exceed the Appalachians, with some 66 percent believing they have qualifications for better jobs. While Appalachians and blacks share similar levels of occupational achievements, many more blacks believe they have unused job skills, and other white migrants and natives of Cincinnati, who already exceed the job attainments of Appalachians, also are more likely to believe they have skills for a better job. White Appalachians are more likely to be found in lower-level occupations and less likely to believe they could do better.

Among those who believe they were qualified for a better job, the jobs white Appalachians believed they were qualified for are of lower status than the jobs people in other groups perceive they are qualified to do. Fifty-six percent

TABLE 3.10

Occupational Qualifications of White Appalachians, White Migrants from Other Areas, White Natives of Cincinnati, and Blacks
(in percent)

Qualification Perception	White Appalachian Migrants	Other White Migrants	Blacks	White Natives
Believe qualified for better job	51	56	66*	58
Job qualified for				
Professional	9	29*	9	15
Managerial	32	56	37	56
Clerical and sales	27	10	24	13
Skilled crafts	9	3	9	8
Semiskilled operatives	15	0	13	0
Service workers	6	3	6	8
Unskilled laborers	3	0	2	0
Number of cases	34	63	46	39
Mean SEI score	44	58*	44	55*

*Significantly different from percentages or average for white Appalachian migrants ($p < .05$).

of the other white migrants and white natives who believed they were qualified for a better job believed they had supervisory or managerial skills, compared to 37 percent of the blacks and 32 percent of the Appalachians; 29 percent of the other white migrants and 15 percent of the white natives believed they had professional skills, but only 9 percent of the blacks and Appalachians believed they did. In total, 85 percent of the other white migrants and 71 percent of the white natives who believed they were qualified for better positions believed they were qualified to do upper-level white-collar jobs, while only 45 percent of the blacks and 41 percent of the Appalachians so perceived themselves. This means that, as a group, Appalachians share the lowest occupational achievements with blacks; are the least likely to perceive themselves as qualified for better jobs; and if they do perceive themselves as qualified for better jobs, are most likely to perceive themselves still qualified only for less prestigious jobs.

A self-fulfilling prophecy may be in operation among white Appalachians. Because they are less likely to perceive that they are qualified for better jobs, they may be less likely to apply for those jobs. If they do not apply for better jobs, they, in turn, will be less likely to obtain those jobs. Blacks, for example, who are the most likely to perceive that they are qualified for better jobs, have also experienced the greatest amount of career mobility. The present generation of Appalachians is unlikely to advance beyond their present occupations, and this means that Appalachians alone may someday hold the unskilled and unrewarding positions.

The conclusion which might be drawn from this picture of Appalachians' experiences in the labor force is mixed. First, Appalachians moved to Cincinnati because of the opportunity to get work. More than any other migrant group, they cited job-related causes as the reasons for moving. They were not attracted by better services, higher welfare benefits, or family, although family reasons might explain their choice of Cincinnati over some other midwestern city. Second, they have been as successful as other white groups in finding work in Cincinnati and more successful than have blacks. This casts doubt on two impressions which exist about Appalachians. First, they do not leave and move back to the mountains whenever they lose their jobs in the cities. Their employment rates are not lower than rates for other white groups, including Cincinnati natives. Second, neither do they form a large pool of unemployed or unemployable people disproportionately burdening the city. They are not more likely than other groups to be out of work. Except for married women whose husbands are employed, Appalachians are as likely to be in the labor force and employed as are other groups. These findings would seem to indicate that Appalachians have assimilated well into the urban labor force.

The job attainments of Appalachian migrants indicate that their assimilation into the urban labor force has been less than perfect. The distribution of the present occupations of Appalachians is similar to that of blacks — disproportionately in lower blue-collar jobs. Other white migrants and white natives of Cincinnati are much more likely to be employed in white-collar jobs or in the higher blue-collar ones. The intergenerational mobility of Appalachians equals that of other white migrants and is greater than that of Cincinnati natives. However, because they started lower, their attainments have not achieved parity with other white groups. The more disturbing factor in the intergenerational mobility of Appalachian migrants is their loss of representation among skilled trades. Appalachians whose fathers were skilled craftsmen have moved into white-collar work, but those whose fathers were in lower blue-collar jobs have not moved into skilled trades. Finally, there is little career mobility among Appalachians, nor are there perceptions that they are qualified for better jobs. The impression that Appalachians take lower-status jobs when first coming to Cincinnati and then work themselves up is not borne out by these data. While other white groups experience a similar lack of career mobility, Appalachians are more likely to believe they are not qualified for better jobs, or, if they do believe they are qualified for better jobs, believe they are qualified for lower jobs than people in other groups believe they are qualified for. Compared to their origins, Appalachians have done well, but compared to other groups, they continue to be at the bottom of the job attainment ladder, with little likelihood of moving up during their lifetimes.

EDUCATIONAL ATTAINMENTS

Formal education is a prerequisite for attainment in many urban occupations. Although education may not be necessary to actually perform the tasks associated with many such jobs, it is often used in screening applicants. Education is taken as an indicator of intelligence, motivation, and character. A person without a formal education may variously be seen as lazy, stupid, or irresponsible, irrespective of what may actually be true.

Appalachian migrants are generally seen as an uneducated people and the participants in this study verify that. Table 3.11 shows that Appalachian migrants have the highest percentage of dropouts before high school graduation, slightly higher than the figure for blacks. Almost half of the Appalachian migrants (46 percent) have less than a high school education, while less than a fourth of the other white migrants and white Cincinnati natives have that little education, 22 percent and 24 percent, respectively. On the other hand, while only 17 percent of Appalachian migrants have any education beyond high school, 50 percent of migrants from other places and 40 percent of the white Cincinnati natives have more than a high school education. The average Appalachian has two years' less education than either other white migrants or white Cincinnati natives. It is clear why in occupational attainments, white Applachians lag so far behind these groups, although it is not clear why their educational attainments are so low.

The educational attainments of white Appalachian migrants are almost identical to those of blacks. The mean amount of education among white

TABLE 3.11
Educational Attainments of White Appalachians, White Migrants from Other Areas, White Natives of Cincinnati, and Blacks
(in percent)

Educational Attainment	White Appalachian Migrants	Other White Migrants	Blacks	White Natives
Less than high school	46	22*	44	24*
High school graduate	36	28	42	35
More than high school	17	50	14	40
Number of Cases	138	199	102	136
Mean years of education	10.8	13.0*	10.7	12.6*

*Significantly different from percentages or average for white Appalachian migrants (p < .05).

Appalachians is 10.8 years and among blacks it is 10.7 years; 46 percent of white Appalachians and 44 percent of blacks have left school before high school graduation; and only 17 percent of white Appalachians and 14 percent of blacks have acquired any additional formal education after high school. With all the attention in the last 25 years that has justifiably been focused upon increasing the educational attainments of blacks, it is at least reasonable to ask why almost no attention has been given to Appalachians.

INCOME ATTAINMENTS

The desire for income is the chief motivating factor in both education and occupation attainment. Table 3.12 shows that the pattern of income distribution is similar to the distributions for both of the other two variables. The median incomes of other white migrants and of white Cincinnati natives are similar to each other, $15,000 and $14,909, respectively, and substantially higher than the incomes of either white Appalachians ($11,250) or blacks ($8,333). More white migrants from places other than Appalachia are found in the upper ranges of the income distribution. Some 39 percent had incomes in 1974 of $18,000 or more, which is more than twice the percentage for white Appalachians (16 percent) and three times the percentage for blacks (11 percent). Although Appalachian migrants have increased their own incomes through migration

TABLE 3.12

Annual Family Income in 1974 of White Appalachians, White Migrants from Other Areas, White Natives of Cincinnati and Blacks (in percent)

Income Distribution	White Appalachian Migrants	Other White Migrants	Blacks	White Natives
Less than $6,000	30	17*	40	11*
$ 6,000 to $11,999	25	21	24	22
$12,000 to $17,999	30	23	25	40
$18,000 and above	16	39	11	26
Number of cases	128	193	91	126
Median income[a]	$11,250	$15,000	$8,333	$14,909

*Significantly different from percentages for white Appalachian migrants (p < .05).

[a]Significance of difference between medians can not be calculated.

and now earn income above that which is typical in the area they left (Morgan, 1981), they continue to earn much less than people who were already in their area of destination or who migrated there from areas outside Appalachia.

The occupational and educational achievements of Appalachians and blacks are more similar than are their incomes. The median income of Appalachians exceeds that of blacks by some $2,917. Further, 40 percent of the blacks, but 30 percent of the Appalachians, have family incomes below $6,000. The sizable income difference in the presence of similar occupational and educational achievements may be due to at least three factors. First, more blacks than Appalachians are unemployed — 90 percent of the Appalachians, but only 63 percent of the blacks, were employed at the time of the survey. While blacks who hold jobs have jobs similar to those of Appalachians, fewer blacks are able to secure employment and that translates into lower income. Second, although blacks and Appalachians have similar occupational attainments, blacks are more frequently found in less financially rewarding positions. For example, 33 percent of employed blacks and 31 percent of employed Appalachians are white-collar workers, but only 14 percent of the blacks, compared to 19 percent of the Appalachians, are professionals or managers. Blacks are also more likely than Appalachians to be working as unskilled laborers. Third, blacks may not receive the same wages as Appalachians when they are employed in the same occupation.

WELFARE DEPENDENCY

Despite the folklore that Appalachians do not receive welfare — even that they go so far as to refuse welfare — 55 percent of the Appalachians in this study either received welfare benefits in the past or were receiving them at the time of the survey. Only the blacks received welfare benefits more frequently than did Appalachians, and both of those groups made greater use of welfare than did either white natives or white migrants from places other than Appalachia. In fact, 20 percent of the Appalachians were receiving some form of welfare benefits at the time of the survey, which is about twice the frequency percentage for migrants from other places (11 percent) or white natives (8 percent), and about half the frequency found among blacks (35 percent).

The most common benefit Appalachians have received is unemployment compensation (42 percent). Instead of depending on their families for support or returning to farm in Appalachia — both widely held impressions — Appalachians who lose their jobs through layoffs and other processes turn to government assistance programs for the unemployed. These benefits provide income which permits them to stay in Cincinnati while they look for new work. In this manner they have become an integrated part of the urban labor force, using resources, within the city, designed to support them when they are forced to look for new jobs. More than any other group, and much more than either white migrants from other places or natives of Cincinnati, white Appalachian migrants receive or have received unemployment compensation.

TABLE 3.13

Welfare Dependency among White Appalachians, White Migrants from Other Areas, White Natives of Cincinnati, and Blacks
(in percent)

Welfare Dependency	White Appalachian Migrants	Other White Migrants	Blacks	White Natives
Present welfare status				
Never received welfare	45	69*	34*	64*
Received welfare in past	35	20	32	29
Presently receiving welfare	20	11	35	8
Number of cases	136	194	98	133
Type of welfare ever received[a]				
Aid to Dependent Children	14	5*	26*	4*
Aid to aged	10	1*	17	2*
Unemployment compensation	42	27*	40	34
Food stamps	22	8*	35*	4*
General welfare	16	4*	23	4*
Other welfare benefits	4	2	10	1
Number of cases	137	200	100	137
Reason for receiving welfare				
Lack of job	72	76	63	87
Lack of spouse	4	11	5	4
Disabled	15	11	27	7
Low income	8	2	5	2
Number of cases	72	54	59	45
Years presently receiving welfare				
Less than one	38	42	26	80
One	19	37	21	0
Two to five	27	21	35	20
More than five	15	0	18	0
Number of cases	26	19	34	10
Mean years	2.9	1.0	3.3	0.4

*Significantly different from percentages for white Appalachian migrants (p $<$ .05).

[a]Significance calculated for each type of welfare received.

41

The second most frequent form of welfare benefits Appalachians have received is food stamps (22 percent). The food stamp program is designed to assist low-income families, including those employed in low-paying jobs, by permitting them to purchase food stamps at a discount. Almost a quarter of the Appalachian families in Cincinnati use or have used this program. Perhaps more than unemployment compensation, dependence on food stamps indicates the degree of acceptance of welfare by Appalachian migrants. Unemployment compensation may be seen as not really welfare, but as a benefit accrued through employment and similar to sick leave or paid vacations. Food stamps are clearly government assistance, however. Appalachians are three times more likely than white migrants from other places, and six times more likely than Cincinnati natives, to have received these benefits. Only blacks receive food stamps more often than do Appalachians.

No other form of government assistance is received by as many as 20 percent of the Appalachian migrants. However, in each case the percentage of Appalachians receiving assistance is greater than the percentages for either white migrants from other areas or Cincinnati natives, and less than the percentage of blacks.

Clearly the impression that Appalachians are reluctant to accept government assistance is not supported by these findings. The rate at which they receive welfare parallels their position in the economic system. Blacks, who have the highest rate of welfare dependency, have the lowest education, the highest unemployment rate, are employed in the lowest-status jobs, and have the lowest incomes. White migrants from outside Appalachia and Cincinnati natives have the lowest rate of welfare dependency and the highest education, occupation, and income attainments. The welfare dependency of Appalachians lies between that of blacks and other whites, which is identical to their relative socioeconomic position.

There has been some speculation that Appalachians who accept welfare would claim physical disabilities. Physical disabilities most clearly remove individuals from responsibility for their situations — they are unable to work. However, only 15 percent of the Appalachians who received welfare benefits claimed physical disabilities. This percentage is higher than among other white groups but is still quite low. A great majority (72 percent) simply state that they were out of work. Appalachians, like other groups, accept unemployment as sufficient justification for public assistance. There appears to be no need to claim physical disability.

The degree of acceptance of welfare on the part of Appalachians is further indicated by the length of time recipients have been using such benefits. White migrants from outside Appalachia and natives of Cincinnati predominantly use welfare benefits for short periods of time: 42 percent of other white migrants and 80 percent of white natives who receive welfare have been receiving benefits for less than a year, an average of 1.0 and 0.4 years, respectively. Appalachians receiving benefits average 2.9 years, which is close to the 3.3-year average among blacks. Only 38 percent of the Appalachians have been receiving welfare less than a year, while 15 percent have been recipients for more than five years. No white migrants from other areas or natives have been receiving assistance for over five years. For at least 15 percent of the Appalachians and 18 percent of the blacks, welfare is no longer a solution to a temporary problem, but is a way of life.

SUMMARY

Living in Cincinnati has been a profitable experience for Appalachians, but not as profitable as it has been for other groups. Most of the Appalachians came to Cincinnati in search of work and most found jobs. Only 6 percent of the Appalachians in the labor force were out of work at the time of the survey, which was the lowest such percentage for any group in Cincinnati. Second, the jobs Appalachians acquired in Cincinnati are generally better than the jobs of their parents: 44 percent of the Appalachians demonstrate upward intergenerational mobility. To some extent, this is an indication that Appalachians found better jobs in the Cincinnati area than they could have expected had they stayed in the Appalachian region. Third, most of the Appalachians have been able to acquire a home in the suburbs: 64 percent of those surveyed were found in suburban neighborhoods; 40 percent had originally settled there, while net outmigration from the inner city added another 24 percent. Clearly, Appalachians are not clustered within inner-city neighborhoods, out of work, with little prospect of a good life. Most have, at some level, achieved the American dream of a good-enough job to provide a home in the suburbs.

Compared to other groups within the Cincinnati area, Appalachians have not done so well. While it is true that they have found work, most are employed only in semiskilled or unskilled jobs. The percentage employed at this level is more than twice the percentage of natives of Cincinnati or of whites from other areas so employed. The occupational distribution of Appalachians is almost identical to that of blacks, but blacks have a much higher unemployment rate (28 percent). It is possible that employers have used Appalachians to meet their need for semiskilled and unskilled laborers in order to deny employment to blacks entirely. Second, although Appalachians have found homes in the suburbs, the neighborhoods where they have moved are working-class, not middle-class ones. Their moves from the inner city to the suburbs have largely been lateral. Third, the incomes of Appalachian families are much lower than those of Cincinnati natives or white migrants from other areas. Almost a third had a total family income in 1974 of less than $6,000.

As a result of their relatively low occupational and income attainments, Appalachians are frequently forced to rely upon government subsidies. Despite the predictions that Appalachians refuse to accept such assistance, only 45 percent of the sample had never used some form of welfare. Most of the users had received unemployment compensation, taking the opportunity to search for new jobs in Cincinnati, instead of returning to Appalachia to await word about available work. Many had also begun to use such programs as food stamps that are designed to offset the effects of low income among the working poor as well as the unemployed.

The outlook for the future attainments of Appalachians in Cincinnati is not good. The educational levels of Appalachians are low: 46 percent left school before high school graduation, the highest percentage of any group, including blacks. The mean amount of education attained among Appalachians is identical to that of blacks. Furthermore, many Appalachians see little possibility that they will advance beyond their present achievements. Fewer Appalachians than any other group believed they were qualified for better jobs. If Appalachians do not believe they are qualified for something better than they have, they will not try to advance, and if they do attempt to move up but lack the necessary skills, their attempts will fail.

4

FROM ONE GENERATION TO THE NEXT

The melting-pot theory has often successfully been used to explain the assimilation of a new group into the dominant culture. It predicts that the first generation of migrants will be upwardly mobile from their points of origin but will not experience levels of attainment equal to those of people already in the area where they moved. Lower levels of education and the necessity of becoming familiar with new surroundings will hinder the occupational and income attainments of the recent migrants. However, because the children of the migrants have an opportunity to obtain an education and acquire other necessary skills, the achievements of the second generation approximate parity with other groups who have been in the area longer. Such a model has predicted, for example, the achievement patterns of European immigrants in the United States, although it does not account for the attainment process among blacks (Blau and Duncan, 1967).

The key indicators necessary to determine if Appalachians are assimilating into the urban environment where they migrated are the relative attainment levels of the second generation of migrants. If the process of assimilation is operating as it should, then the attainments of the second generation of Appalachians should be higher than the attainments of the first generation and approximately the same as those of the second generation of migrants from other areas and people who have lived in the Cincinnati area for longer periods of time. The comparison of first- and second-generation migrants is not the same as the comparison of parents and children. It has already been shown in Chapter 2 that the two generations of Appalachians are approximately the same age. The point of the comparison is to determine if those factors which are responsible for the lower attainments of Appalachians disappear from one generation to the next, as would be expected if Appalachians are assimilating into the areas where they migrated.

One word of caution: Dividing the groups into first- and second-generation migrants leaves rather large room for error in comparing one group to another. Only very large differences will be statistically significant. The findings in this chapter can therefore be only suggestive of the differences which exist in each generation.

HOUSING PATTERNS

Instead of showing neighborhoods approaching similarity with those of people who are native to the Cincinnati area, data on housing patterns indicate that Appalachians in the second generation lag further behind the attainments of natives. Table 4.1 shows that the median incomes of the neighborhoods in which second-generation Appalachians are living are lower than the neighborhood incomes of first-generation Appalachians and consequently lower than the neighborhood incomes of white natives. Half of the Appalachians who are first-generation migrants live in neighborhoods which have median incomes of $10,526 or more. The median neighborhood income of second-generation migrants is $10,166, or $360 less. Instead of neighborhood incomes becoming more similar to those of white natives in Cincinnati, the difference has increased from $514 to $874, or by more than half again the original difference.

Second-generation white migrants from places other than Appalachia also live in neighborhoods with lower median incomes than the first generation does. The second generation shows a drop of $743 to $11,333. However, both first- and second-generation white migrants from outside Appalachia live in neighborhoods with higher incomes than white natives, which in turn are higher than the incomes of neighborhoods where either white Appalachians or blacks are found. The decline shown by second-generation white migrants from outside Appalachia reflects a loss of an initial advantage which such migrants had and shows a process of their becoming similar to people who have lived in Cincinnati for at least three generations.

Blacks show an improvement in the incomes of neighborhoods between first and second generations. The first generation lives in neighborhoods with median incomes of $8,000, while the cutoff point for the second generation climbs slightly to $8,250. Perhaps the attempt to improve the quality of housing among blacks is having an effect, although not a miraculous one. Both groups of blacks remain at the bottom of the scale of housing attainments.

A much higher percentage of second-generation white Appalachians than of the first live in the inner city of Cincinnati. Remembering, from Chapter 3, that many Appalachians first settled in the inner city and subsequently moved to the suburbs, these data would seem to indicate that such moves were possible for first-generation Appalachians, but the second generation has not been able

TABLE 4.1
Housing Patterns of White Appalachians, White Migrants from Other Areas, and Blacks, by First- and Second-Generation Migrant Status

Housing Pattern	White Appalachians		Other White Migrants		Blacks		White Natives
	First	Second	First	Second	First	Second	
Median median income of neighborhood[a]	$10,526	$10,166	$12,076	$11,333	$8,000	$8,250	$11,040
Percent in inner city	30	45	38	41	84*	84**	48*
Number of cases	80	56	114	87	56	37	137

*Significantly different from percentages for first-generation Appalachian migrants (p <.05).
**Significantly different from percentages for second-generation Appalachian migrants (p <.05).

[a]Significance of difference between medians can not be calculated.

to repeat the experience. Perhaps even better than the income of neighborhoods, the failure of second-generation Appalachians to migrate to the suburbs indicates the failure of housing attainments to increase from the first generation to the next, instead showing a decline. The percentages of white migrants from other areas and blacks who live in the inner city have remained stable between generations.

The percentage of natives living within the city limits of Cincinnati is higher than that of either Appalachians or white migrants from other areas. Cincinnati is a city of neighborhoods and perhaps these people chose to continue to live in the same neighborhoods from generation to generation. Many of Cincinnati's neighborhoods are very nice places to live. Perhaps white natives are clustering into those places. The median incomes of the neighborhoods where they live would seem to indicate that. In any case, there is no reason to believe that they could not move to the suburbs if that were their desire.

OCCUPATIONAL ATTAINMENTS

The unemployment rate shows a major difference between the first and second generation of Appalachian migrants. First-generation migrants have the lowest unemployment rate (3 percent) of any group, while second-generation migrants have a rate (11 percent) which is higher than any of the other groups, except blacks. Both generations of white migrants from other areas and people who have lived in the area longer have higher unemployment rates than do first-generation Appalachians, but lower unemployment rates than does the second generation. The concept of the stem-family that is often applied to Appalachian migrants posits that Appalachians return to Appalachia when work is unavailable in the city. Such a pattern may be true for first-generation migrants, for it appears that their unemployment rate is well below the level of other groups. Second-generation migrants, on the other hand, do not have that option open to them. Their family ties are in the city, not in Appalachia, and they therefore do not have the option of returning to Appalachia when work is lacking in the city. They remain in the city and their unemployment rate becomes high.

While the unemployment rate of second-generation Appalachians is higher than that of the first generation, their occupational distributions are almost identical. The second generation has not been able to move out of the semi-skilled and unskilled positions their parents acquired upon first moving to Cincinnati. It has been held that Appalachia did not provide sufficient educational opportunities for migrants to receive the training necessary for either white-collar positions or skilled crafts. The migrants were thought to be further hindered by socialization in a rural instead of an urban environment (Philliber, 1981). Neither of those explanations applies to second-generation Appalachians. They were raised in an urban area where educational opportunities were available. Despite those factors, they have not risen above the level of attainments achieved by the first generation of Appalachians in the city.

TABLE 4.2
Occupational Attainments of White Appalachians, White Migrants from Other Areas, and Blacks, by First- and Second-Generation Migrant Status
(in percent)

Occupational Attainment	White Appalachians		Other White Migrants		Blacks		White Natives
	First	Second	First	Second	First	Second	
Percent of labor force unemployed	3	11	9	6	26*	31	8
Number of cases	37	28	69	52	34	26	88
Occupational distribution							
Professional/managerial	18	18	54*	32**	18	8	30**
Clerical/sales	12	12	15	27	9	29	31
Skilled crafts	14	12	16	9	13	4	16
Semiskilled and unskilled	55	58	15	22	60	58	23
Number of cases	49	33	80	63	45	24	97
Mean SEI score	32	33	55*	45**	30	30	44**
Believe qualified for better job	45	60	56	56	51	89**	58
Number of cases	44	35	75	62	45	27	95

*Significantly different from percentages or averages for first-generation Appalachian migrants (p < .05).
**Significantly different from percentages or averages for second-generation Appalachian migrants (p < .05).

The second generation of white migrants from places other than Appalachia shows a decline in occupational achievements. There is a sizable decrease in the proportions holding professional/managerial positions or holding jobs in skilled trades. As a result of the decline, the second generation of whites who migrated from other areas has levels of attainment approximately the same as natives of the area. The first generation of migrants from outside Appalachia had a disproportionate number in professional and managerial posts. They were recruited to Cincinnati by employers seeking their skills. Their children have assimilated into the labor force such that they are at parity with people whose families have been there longer.

Blacks show an increased representation among lower white-collar workers. Those positions were the early targets of civil rights demonstrations; pressure was created to hire blacks as clerks and salespersons as well as office workers. As a result, the second generation of blacks in Cincinnati has a greater representation among white-collar workers. At the same time, blacks show a decline in representation among professionals and managerial workers and in skilled trades. Despite efforts to increase the representation of black administrators and black craftsmen, the second generation in Cincinnati has done less well than the first. Perhaps white administrators are willing to hire blacks as lower white-collar workers but not as coworkers, and perhaps trade unions continue to exclude blacks from skilled trades.

Appalachians do not appear to be assimilating into the labor force of the Cincinnati area. The second-generation Appalachians have occupational achievements no higher than those of the first generation, which are much lower than the occupational achievements of natives and of migrants from other areas. Furthermore, the rate of unemployment shows an increase from the first generation to the second that is almost four times greater in the second generation. The occupational distribution of either generation of Appalachians is highly similar to that of blacks, and the ability of the assimilation hypothesis to predict the occupational attainments is no greater for Appalachians than it is for blacks. The failure to approach parity with whites native to the area, in terms of occupational achievements, may be as strong a basis for ethnic-group formation among Appalachians as it has been for blacks.

The comparisons of Appalachians and other groups in Cincinnati, shown in Chapter 3, indicated that Appalachians were relatively satisfied with their occupational attainments. Fewer Appalachians than other groups believed they were qualified for jobs which were better than the ones they presently held. Such a statement is true for the first generation of migrants but not for the second. The only group in which a higher proportion believe that they are qualified for better jobs than they have is the second generation of blacks. More second-generation Appalachians believe they are qualified for better jobs than do any of the other white groups. First-generation migrants could compare their attainments to what they could have expected had they stayed in Appalachia, and might find that they are doing better. Second-generation migrants can compare themselves to their parents or to other people who were raised in Cincinnati, but they are unlikely to compare themselves to people living in Appalachia. When they compare themselves to their reference groups, they will find they are doing no better than their parents, and worse than other people with whom they were raised. As a result, 60 percent believe they should have better jobs than they presently have. This may indicate the beginning of feelings of antagonism among Appalachians.

EDUCATIONAL ATTAINMENTS

The comparison between generations shows an improvement in the educational attainments of Appalachians. The percentage leaving before completing high school drops from 50 percent to 41 percent and the percentage going beyond high school increases from 15 percent to 21 percent. As a result, the average number of years of education completed increases from 10.6 for the first generation to 11.2 for the second, an increase of a little over half a year in a single generation. This would seem to indicate that Appalachians are taking advantage of the opportunities available to secure the training necessary for employment in urban areas.

The comparison of Appalachians and other groups shows a different picture. Second-generation Appalachians have higher failure rates in completion of high school than similar generations of other white migrants or blacks and a much higher rate than Cincinnati natives. While as a total group, the educational attainments of blacks are lower than Appalachians', the second generation of blacks averages a full year more of education than does the first generation. As a result, blacks and Appalachians in the second generation in Cincinnati have equal educational attainments. Both groups continue to lag behind the attainments of other white migrants or white Cincinnati natives. If present trends continue, it will not be long before Appalachians are alone at the bottom of the educational attainment ladder. While it is true that their levels of educational attainments are increasing, at the present rate it will be several generations before parity is achieved with natives in the area. For blacks, parity is a reasonable expectation in the next generation as long as present trends continue.

The second generation of migrants from areas outside Appalachia shows the same pattern of decrease found among both housing and occupational attainments. Second-generation migrants from other areas have less education than the first generation and approximately the same level of education as natives of the Cincinnati area. On this indicator, as well as the others, white migrants from places other than Appalachia are merging with white Cincinnati natives into a single group. Only blacks and white Appalachians remain outside as separate groups for longer than the passing of a single generation.

The prognosis for the educational attainments of future generations of Appalachians is not good. Participants in this study were asked about the number

TABLE 4.3
Educational Attainments of White Appalachians, White Migrants from Other Areas, and Blacks, by First- and Second-Generation Migrant Status

(in percent)

Educational Attainment	White Appalachians		Other White Migrants		Blacks		White Natives
	First	Second	First	Second	First	Second	
Less than high school	50	41	15*	31	48	38	24** *
High school graduate	35	38	24	33	39	49	35
More than high school	15	21	61	36	12	14	40
Number of cases	80	56	113	86	56	37	136
Mean years of education	10.6	11.2	13.5*	12.3**	10.2	11.2	12.6** *

*Significantly different from percentages or averages for first-generation Appalachian migrants (p <.05).
**Significantly different from percentages or averages for second-generation Appalachian migrants (p <.05).

TABLE 4.4
Educational Aspirations for Children of White Appalachians, White Migrants from Other Areas, and Blacks, by First- and Second-Generation Migrant Status

Aspiration	White Appalachians		Other White Migrants		Blacks		White Natives
	First	Second	First	Second	First	Second	
Percent desiring more than high school education for child	69	54	77	68	85	83**	67
Number of cases	49	37	65	37	33	24	61

**Significantly different from percentages for second-generation Appalachian migrants (p < .05).

of years of education they would like to see their children obtain. Table 4.4 shows the percentage of each group wanting more than a high school education for their children. The second generation of Appalachians has the lowest percentage wanting more than a high school education for their children. Blacks have the highest percentage, followed by white migrants from areas other than Appalachia and natives of Cincinnati. Many children continue in school because of the urging of their parents. If fewer Appalachians want their children to continue, then they are less likely to attempt to influence their children in that direction. As a result, the rate at which Appalachians are closing the gap between their educational attainments and the attainments of natives in the area may decrease and, as a result, never achieve parity.

INCOME ATTAINMENTS

Generational differences in the income attainments of Appalachians parallel the data for housing, jobs, and education. Little income difference exists between first- and second-generation Appalachians. The median family income for each group is $11,250. There is some improvement in the second generation, as indicated by the percentages of low-income families: 34 percent of the first generation, but only 25 percent of the second, have family incomes below $6,000. Both generations have incomes below those of either white migrants from places other than Appalachia or Cincinnati natives. There would appear to be little evidence from their income attainments that Appalachians are assimilating into the Cincinnati area.

The second generation of white migrants from places outside Appalachia again shows a lower level of attainment than did the first generation. However, instead of achieving the same level of income as Cincinnati natives, the second-generation migrants from outside Appalachia have a median income that is $2,909 less than Cincinnati natives and a much higher percentage of families below the $6,000 mark. While the other measures of attainment have consistently shown the attainment of parity in the second generation among these migrants, income attainment falls below the level of Cincinnati natives. Given the pattern of other dimensions of achievement, perhaps this finding can be dismissed as an error in the data.

The second generation of blacks in Cincinnati also shows a decline in income attainment: The median family income decreases by $2,234. While the percentage of families below the $6,000 level does not increase, the percentage of upper-income blacks decreases. This is probably the result of the occupational redistribution between generations. While the overall level remained the same, fewer blacks were in skilled trades or professional/managerial positions. It is these positions which are better-paying ones. As a result of the loss of representation in those occupations, the income level of the second-generation blacks in Cincinnati is lower than that of the first.

TABLE 4.5
Income Attainments of White Appalachians, White Migrants from Other Areas, and Blacks, by First- and Second-Generation Migrant Status

Attainment	White Appalachians		Other White Migrants		Blacks		White Natives
	First	Second	First	Second	First	Second	
Median family income[a]	$11,250	$11,250	$18,636	$12,000	$9,400	$7,166	$14,909*
Percent below $6,000	34	25	13*	21	38	41	12**
Number of cases	71	55	108	85	48	34	126

*Significantly different from percentages for first-generation Appalachian migrants (p <.05).
**Significantly different from percentages for second-generation Appalachian migrants (p <.05).

a Significance of difference between medians can not be calculated.

CONCLUSIONS

The comparison of the socioeconomic attainments of first- and second-generation migrants would seem to indicate that Appalachians are not assimilating into the Cincinnati community. Instead, they demonstrate a pattern similar to that found among blacks. Second-generation Appalachians show no improvement in housing or occupations and little improvement in educational attainment or income. They are more likely to be unemployed and to believe that they are qualified for a better job than they have. If assimilation is seen as approaching parity with the community from one generation to the next, then Appalachians are little more assimilated into Cincinnati now than they were when first coming to the area.

Blacks also show little movement toward assimilation into the Cincinnati community and remain far from the attainment of parity. The second generation ranks higher than the first in educational attainments and in educational aspirations for their children. However, both generations live in the same level of neighborhoods and work at approximately the same types of jobs, and the first generation has the higher median income of the two groups.

Only white migrants who came to Cincinnati from places other than Appalachia show assimilation into the Cincinnati community, and it is almost total by the second generation. The second generation white non-Appalachian migrants live in approximately the same level of neighborhood, work in the same types of jobs, and have approximately the same educational attainments as do Cincinnati natives. The data do show lower income attainments for second-generation, white non-Appalachian migrants, but even on that measure they are closer to Cincinnati natives than is any other group.

5

DIFFERENT RESOURCES, DIFFERENT PAYOFFS

In the general population, the most central variable in socioeconomic attainment is an individual's occupation, and the most critical variables determining an individual's occupation are family background, education, and work experience (Blau and Duncan, 1967). The lower attainments of Appalachians may occur because they have backgrounds which provide them with fewer resources with which to obtain socioeconomic success in urban areas. They come from families which, by U.S. standards, are poor. They lack the education which is a necessary prerequisite for many better-paying jobs. The work experience they have is often irrelevant to urban occupations. Knowing the mechanics of coal mining, timber extraction, or farming has little utility in work in cities. It may well be that the same factors which determine socioeconomic attainment in the general population are what determine socioeconomic attainment among Appalachians, and that Appalachians have lower attainments only because they have fewer resources.

It is possible that there are factors unique to Appalachians which affect their socioeconomic attainments. Family relationships and Appalachian cultural values are often cited as two such variables. Strong family ties have been cited as assisting socioeconomic attainments among Appalachians (Brown, 1968; Schwarzweller and Seggar, 1967). They provide information about jobs, housing for new migrants searching for work, and assistance in adjusting to the city. Appalachian cultural values, on the other hand, are more often cited as hindering assimilation (Giffin, 1956; Ergood, 1976). Values such as independence make it difficult to work for other people; fatalism makes it difficult to try to better one's situation; and traditionalism makes it difficult to change. It may well be that these factors are unique to Appalachians and are factors in their socioeconomic achievements.

A third possibility is that the same variables which determine the socio-economic achievements of the general population also determine the socioeconomic attainments of Appalachians, but that Appalachians fail to receive the same payoffs for resources that other groups receive. For example, a person with a college education expects to obtain a certain level of occupation. It could be possible that Appalachians who obtain a college education are not able to get the type of job they expect. Such could occur because of inferior-quality schools, lack of knowledge about how to get an upper-white-collar job, or discrimination.

The three explanations have different implications for understanding the relative attainments of Appalachians. The first model, which parallels predictions of the melting-pot theory, holds that the same explanations for socioeconomic attainment in the general population are appropriate for Appalachians. As the backgrounds of Appalachians improve, the socioeconomic attainments of Appalachians are expected to approach parity with the general population. Lower educational attainments, poorer families, and little experience in cities are held to account for the present relatively low standing of Appalachians. The second model, derived from the theory of cultural conflict, predicts that additional variables are necessary to account for the socioeconomic attainments of Appalachians. Values and cultural traits common among Appalachian people hinder their ability to compete for socioeconomic rewards in an environment unappreciative of their character. If resources were equalized, Appalachians who hold those values would still have lower socioeconomic attainments. The third model emphasizes the payoffs received for resources. The variables which influence attainments of the general population may not affect Appalachians in the same way. If resources were equalized, Appalachians would still not have the same attainments of the general population because the payoffs for those resources are not the same. These lower payoffs could result from inexperience in converting resources into achievements or from discrimination. In this chapter the importance of each of these models in understanding the relative educational, occupational, and income attainments of Appalachians will be studied.

The attainment process among Appalachians will be compared to that of whites who have lived in the Cincinnati area for at least three generations, of white migrants from places other than Appalachia, and of blacks. The attainment processes of white natives and white migrants from places other than Appalachia are expected to be similar to each other. The attainment process of blacks has previously been found to be different (Coleman, Berry, and Blum, 1972; Blum, 1972; Coleman, Blum, Sorensen, and Rossi, 1972). Not only are the resources of blacks lower than those of whites; the payoffs whites receive for their resources are different. By comparing Appalachians with each of these groups, it will be possible to determine if the attainment process among Appalachians is similar to that of other whites, similar to that of blacks, or different from both.

INCOME ATTAINMENT

For most families, the primary source of income is the category of wages and salaries paid to the heads of households for performance in an occupational position. In general, the higher the status of the occupation, the higher the earnings. The occupational status of the head of household was determined by the occupation of the husband, if the person was married, or the respondent, male or female, if the person was not married. Occupations were classified by using the U.S. Bureau of the Census's *Index of Occupations and Industries* (1972) and transforming the classifications into Duncan SEI scores.

Education may have a secondary effect upon earnings. Two persons doing identical work may not be paid the same because of differences in their educational attainments. The better-educated workers may be paid more because they have invested more in training, or they may be paid less either because they are new workers obtaining experience necessary for promotion to a better job or because they have chosen a career which offers little pay but other rewards, such as school teaching or social work. Education was measured by the number of years of school the individual had completed.

In order for occupational status or education to have a payoff in earnings, the individual must have a job. The employment status of the head of household was determined by whether the head was employed full time or part time at the time of the interview.

In many families where both the husband and the wife are present, the family income is higher because both partners work. The contribution of the wife to family income was determined by whether the head of household had a wife who participated in the labor force.

Table 5.1 presents the standardized regression coefficients for the effects of these four variables on the income attainment process of Appalachians. Standardized regression coefficients are used to determine which variables are the most important within a population. The greater the absolute value of a coefficient, the more important the variable is. A common convention is to

TABLE 5.1
Relative Effects of Determinants of Family
Income among Appalachians
(standardized regression coefficients)

Predictor Variable	β
Employment of head of household	.31
Education of head of household	.35
Occupational SEI score of head of household	.05
Employment of wife	.08

consider coefficients less than .10 as unimportant. Table 5.1 indicates that the education and employment of the head of household are the two most important variables in the income attainment process of Appalachians.

Independent of other factors, the higher the educational attainment of the head of household in an Appalachian family, the higher the family income. Education was expected to have less of an effect than occupational status, but, for Appalachian heads of households, the effect of education is seven times as great. Although in the general population, education is used to obtain an occupation and income is primarily based upon occupational status, it appears that among Appalachian heads of households, education is directly converted into income.

The employment status of the head of household is almost as important as his education in determining family income. As observed in Chapter 3, most Appalachian families depend upon the husband to be the sole provider; only about a third of the wives studied participated in the labor force. As a result, if the head of household loses his job, becomes disabled, or retires, it makes a major difference in the income of the family. Among groups with more dual-worker families, or where the wife frequently earned most of the family income, the failure of the husband to be employed would have less of an effect upon their standard of living.

The occupational status of the head of household is not very important in the income attainment process among Appalachians. This is perhaps because so many hold lower blue-collar jobs with little variability in earnings. What is important is whether the head of household has a job. Appalachian families in which the head of household is employed earn more than families in which the head is not.

Once the head of household's employment status, education, and occupational status have been taken into account, the wife's employment status adds little to the prediction of family income. Because only a small minority live in dual-worker families, employment of the wife is not important in understanding differences in income among Appalachians.

Two different kinds of comparisons are important in trying to determine why the incomes of Appalachians are different from those of other groups. Do Appalachians differ in the levels of those variables which affect income and do Appalachians differ in how those variables affect income? The answer to the first question is found by comparing the means of the independent variables in the income attainment process. The answer to the second question is found by comparing the unstandardized regression coefficients. Unstandardized regression coefficients indicate how much difference exists in the dependent variable (income) as the result of a difference in one unit of a given independent variable (a year of education, for example).

Table 5.2 presents a comparison of the means of the independent variables in the income attainment process. In general it can be seen that Appalachians are lower on these variables than are other white migrants or natives of the

TABLE 5.2
Means of Determinants of Family Income

Predictor Variable	White Appalachian Migrant	Other White Migrant	Black	White Cincinnati Native
Head of household				
Employment status	0.67	0.70	0.54*	0.74
Education	10.91	13.19*	10.49	12.74*
Occupational SEI	36.80	52.53*	35.19	43.51*
Wife's employment status	0.22	0.33*	0.30	0.30
Income	$11,867	$15,878*	$9,560*	$14,877*

*Significantly different from means for white Appalachian migrants ($p < .05$).

Cincinnati area and are approximately the same as are blacks. Approximately the same percentage of Appalachian heads of households are employed as are white migrants from other areas or Cincinnati natives — which is considerably above the employment rate of blacks. However, in terms of either educational attainment or occupational status, Appalachian heads of households and black heads of households are approximately the same and substantially below white natives or migrants from other areas. Except for the higher employment rates of Appalachians, Appalachian and black heads of households are alike and different from other whites.

The probability of being married and living in a family where the wife works is lower among Appalachians than among any of the other groups. Only 22 percent of the Appalachians lived in such a family. The literature on the traditional organization of the Appalachian family is extensive. In the traditional family, the male head of household performs the sole provider role while the wife tends to the house and children. It would appear that this pattern continues to be the predominant form of family organization among Appalachians, even after migration.

The effects of these different variables may be seen in Table 5.3. The data would seem to indicate that the process of income attainment for Appalachians is not the same as it is for other groups. Appalachians receive approximately the same payoff as other groups for employment of the head of household, but for other variables, the payoff is different. In all four groups, employment of the head of household increases the family income by approximately $5,000. Payoff is highest for other white migrants ($5,211) and lowest for Cincinnati natives ($4,480), with Appalachians approximately in the middle ($4,992).

Education is more important to the income attainment of Appalachians than to people in any of the other groups. For each year of education an

TABLE 5.3
Comparative Effects of Determinants of Family Income
(unstandardized regression coefficients)

Predictor Variable	White Appalachian Migrant	Other White Migrant	Black	White Cincinnati Native
Head of household				
Employment status	$4,992	$5,211	$4,706	$4,480
Education	877	514	340	310
Occupational SEI	17	72	38	72
Wife's employment status	1,400	4,214	5,686	1,610
Intercept	−1,989	287	371	4,022

Appalachian receives, he can expect an additional $877 in family income. This is considerably more than the payoff for other white migrants ($514) and more than twice the payoff for blacks ($340) and Cincinnati natives ($310). On the one hand, this may be taken as evidence that Appalachians benefit more from attainment of higher education than do people in other groups, but, on the other hand, it also indicates that the failure to obtain a high education is more problematic for Appalachians than for others. It has previously been noted that the average Appalachian has less than 11 years of schooling; 46 percent failed to complete high school, and only 17 percent have any education beyond high school. The 17 percent who obtained some years of college have perhaps been able to compete favorably with other people, but the 83 percent who are not as fortunate have not fared as well. It cost these Appalachians $877 for each year of school they failed to get, which is $367 more than it cost other migrants and more than $500 greater than the cost incurred either by blacks or by Cincinnati natives.

Appalachians receive the lowest payoff, for each increase in occupational status, of any group. Blacks receive twice the payoff as Appalachians ($38 compared to $17), and other white migrants and white Cincinnati natives receive more than four times as much ($72). This difference may be due to a number of factors. First, the payoff for higher-status occupations often comes after years of work, while the top in lower-status occupations is reached quickly. Those Appalachians who hold managerial and professional positions may be young. If so, their incomes would not be much higher than the incomes of semi-skilled and skilled workers with a number of years of experience. As these Appalachians establish their careers, their incomes may be expected to rise for a number of years to come. Second, Appalachians who are employed in higher-status positions may be employed in lower-paying positions than are people in other groups. For example, the Appalachian may have a lower-management job and the other migrant an upper-management one. Both would have the same SEI score but the other migrant would have a substantially higher salary. Third, Appalachians may accept jobs with relatively high starting salaries but with little promise of advancement. If a person fears discrimination or, for some other reason, believes he cannot depend on receiving raises over a number of years, then it is important to initially obtain the highest-paying job an individual can obtain. This pattern has been shown to exist among blacks in the general population (Blum, 1972). It appears to be even stronger among Appalachians. White migrants from outside Appalachia and natives of the Cincinnati area appear to seek the highest-status position that they can obtain and receive increments in income over a long period of time. Blacks and especially Appalachians appear reluctant to take such a risk and exchange education for immediate income.

The wife's employment status contributes less to the family income of Appalachians than among any other group, and substantially less than among either other white migrants or blacks. The husband is the sole provider in most Appalachian families. Those wives who work have few job skills which would enable them to take good-paying jobs. Black wives, who contribute the greatest benefit to their families from their employment, also have few job skills, but fewer of their husbands are employed. As a result, their families are more dependent upon their earnings and the payoff from the wife's employment is greater. It is among other white migrants that one is most likely to find wives working at higher-paying jobs resulting in a sizable increment in family income.

The importance of the observed differences in resources and differences in effects of these resources can be determined by using the average resources of one group and the unstandardized regression coefficients of another group. To see how Appalachians would do if they had the resources of other groups, the average level of resources of each of the other groups is substituted into the regression equation for income attainment of Appalachians and the expected income is estimated. Thus the equation becomes:

$$\overline{Y} = a + b_1\overline{X}_1 + b_2\overline{X}_2 + b_3\overline{X}_3 + b_4\overline{X}_4$$

where $\overline{Y}$ = estimated average income using resources of other group

a = estimated Appalachian income with other factors equal to zero

b_1 = effect of head's employment status among Appalachians

$\overline{X}_1$ = average of head's employment status in reference group

b_2 = effect of head's education among Appalachians

$\overline{X}_2$ = average head's education in reference group

b_3 = effect of head's SEI among Appalachians

$\overline{X}_3$ = average head's SEI in reference group

b_4 = effect of wife's employment status among Appalachians

$\overline{X}_4$ = average wife's employment status in reference group

TABLE 5.4
Predicted Income of Appalachians, Based upon Levels of Resources and Efficacy of Resources Found in Reference Groups

	Predicted Income of Appalachians	
Reference Group	*Appalachian efficacy; Reference-Group Resources*	*Appalachian resources; Reference-Group Efficacy*
Appalachians	$11,867	$11,867
Other white migrants	$14,428	$12,941
Blacks	$10,928	$ 9,882
Natives	$14,038	$13,410

This equation was calculated by using the average of the independent variables of each of the other groups to estimate what the average income of Appalachians would be if they had the resources of other groups. These figures are presented in the first column of Table 5.4.

The data indicate that the average family income of Appalachians would be improved if they had the average resources of either other white migrants or Cincinnati natives; or, stated differently, Appalachians are seen to have fewer resources which can be converted to income. It is easy to see why Appalachians would do better if they had the average characteristics of white migrants from other areas or natives of Cincinnati. Both groups rank higher on every determinant of family income. They have higher rates of employment, higher educational attainments, higher occupational achievements, and more frequently live in households where both the husband and the wife are employed. If Appalachians had the same characteristics as white migrants from other areas, their average income would be expected to increase by $2,561, to $14,428, and if they had the same characteristics as Cincinnati natives, their income would be expected to increase by $2,171, to $14,038.

Appalachians would have lower family incomes, by $939, if they had the resources of blacks. While blacks are more likely to live in families in which the wife is employed, the black head of household is less likely to be employed than is the head of household of an Appalachian family. In addition, the black head of household has slightly less education and, if employed, is employed in a job with slightly lower status than is the Appalachian head of household. These characteristics of the head of household more than offset the increases in family income which result from the more frequent employment of the wife.

The unstandardized regression coefficients indicate the rate at which resources are converted into income. To see how Appalachians would fare if they converted resources into income at the same rate as do other groups, estimated income is determined by pairing the average resources of Appalachians with the unstandardized regression coefficients of a comparison group. Thus the equation becomes:

$$\overline{Y} = a + b_1\overline{X}_1 + b_2\overline{X}_2 + b_3\overline{X}_3 + b_4\overline{X}_4$$

where $\overline{Y}$ = estimated income using conversion rate of other group

a = estimated reference group income with other factors equal to zero

b_1 = effect of head's employment status among reference group

$\overline{X}_1$ = average head's employment status among Appalachians

b_2 = effect of head's education among reference group

$\overline{X}_2$ = average head's education among Appalachians

b_3 = effect of head's SEI among reference group

$\overline{X}_3$ = average head's SEI among Appalachians

b_4 = effect of wife's employment status among reference group

$\overline{X}_4$ = average wife's employment status among Appalachians

This equation was calculated with the conversion rate of the independent variables of each of the other groups, to estimate what the average income of Appalachians would be if they converted resources to income at the same rate as do other groups. These figures are presented in the final column of Table 5.4.

The comparison of these figures indicates that Appalachians convert resources into income differently from other groups. If the attainment model for Appalachians were the same as for other white migrants, Appalachians could expect an average family income of $12,941, or $1,074 more than they presently earn. If their attainment process were the same as for Cincinnati natives, they could expect an average family income of $13,410, or an increment of $1,543. Appalachians pay a higher price than either of these groups for the failure to have resources which can be converted into income. For example, if a family has an employed head of household with a college education (16 years) and a good job (status score of 75) and a wife who does not participate in the labor force, the family can expect to have an income of $18,310, if the people are Appalachians; $19,122, if they are other white migrants; and $18,862, if they are Cincinnati natives. While the Appalachian family would still receive less, the income would be $812 lower than that of other white migrants and only $552 lower than that of Cincinnati natives. However, if a family has an unemployed head of household with only an eighth-grade education and a semi-skilled job (status score of 25) and a wife who does not participate in the labor force, the family can expect to have an income of $10,444, if the people are Appalachians; $11,410, if they are other white migrants; and $12,782, if they are Cincinnati natives. The difference in family income increases slightly to $966 for other white migrants but increases substantially to $2,338 for Cincinnati natives. The primary determinants of income among Appalachians are the head's employment and education. The payoff for employment is about the same as for other groups, but the payoff for education is much higher. While an educated Appalachian employed in a good job competes well for income with similar people in other groups, the uneducated Appalachian does not. If a person is uneducated, it helps very much to be a Cincinnati native.

Blacks, who have similar levels of education as Appalachians, do not appear to convert the attainment of education into income as Appalachians are able to do. As a result, if Appalachians converted resources into income according to the model for blacks, they would have an average income of $9,882, or a loss of $1,985. This may indicate that Appalachians who acquire a college education and good jobs compete favorably with other whites for income, but that blacks with similar resources continue to be left out.

These findings indicate that Appalachians have lower family incomes than other white groups both because they have fewer resources which can be converted into income and because the process of conversion is different for them. Of these two sets of factors, the difference in resources appears to be the more important. Appalachians have lower family incomes because they average fewer years of education, have lower job attainments, and less often are living in households where the wife is employed. If their averages on these variables were the same as averages of other white migrants, they would be expected to have an income $2,561 higher than observed, and if they had the same averages as Cincinnati natives, they would be expected to have an income $2,171 higher than observed.

Differences in the conversion of resources into income suggest that Appalachians who are well educated and have good jobs are assimilated into the competition for income with other whites, but that Appalachians who lack these advantages pay a higher price for it than other people. If the process of attainment for Appalachians were the same as it is for other white migrants, Appalachians could expect an additional $1,074 in average family income, and if the process were the same as for Cincinnati natives, they could expect an additional $1,543. Because most Appalachians do not have a college education and professional and managerial jobs, they are at a disadvantage in the competition with other people who also lack these advantages but are not penalized as Appalachians are.

OCCUPATIONAL ATTAINMENT

While income is a family characteristic shared by people living together as a unit, occupational attainment is a characteristic of an individual. The comparison of the determination of occupational attainments among Appalachians and of that among other groups is appropriately based upon the attainments of those participants who were employed at the time of the survey or upon the last occupation of those who had previously worked but were presently unemployed, disabled, or retired. Occupational attainments were again ranked by Duncan SEI scores.

The process of occupational attainment in the general population primarily derives from educational attainment and family background (Blau and Duncan, 1967). To compare the effects of these on the attainments of Appalachians and other groups, education was measured again by years of school completed. The socioeconomic status of the family of origin was measured by the occupational status held by the head of household in the home where the individual was raised.

A third background measure relevant to differences in the occupational attainments of Appalachians and others is the size of the place where the person was raised. Several times it has been intimated that Appalachians do not obtain much occupational success in the cities where they migrated because they have come from rural areas, where the experiences obtained have little relevance to urban occupations (Philliber, 1981). Knowing how to farm, mine coal, or cut timber is not particularly useful to employers in the city. Participants were therefore classified by whether they were raised in a rural area, in a town of less than 25,000 people, in a small city of between 25,000 and 100,000, or in a metropolitan area of more than 100,000.

Involvement in an extended family system has often been cited as a distinguishing characteristic of Appalachians. Migrants are said to choose their cities of destination because relatives are located there (Brown, 1968); to find jobs through contacts these relatives provide (Brown, 1968; Schwarzweller, 1981); and to maintain contacts with relatives still living in Appalachia, through frequent visits (Brown, 1968). While family members may provide assistance in locating work, they may inadvertently limit the occupational attainment of the person they so aid. In effect, the occupation of the person who finds work for a relative is the top occupation the relative can expect. If the person were able to find a higher-status job for someone else, it is only reasonable to assume that that person would take the job himself. In order to get a better job than relatives have, it is necessary to use some other source. Persons who acquire jobs through the help of relatives consequently will be expected to have lower average attainments than other people. In this study, dependence upon family was measured by whether the individual moved to Cincinnati because family members were already there and by whether they had obtained their jobs through help from relatives.

Individuals who frequently leave town to visit relatives may also limit their occupational attainments. If a person is frequently out of town, for example, that person has less time to make friends and socialize with co-workers who could be important in future promotion decisions. An employer might take such behavior as an indication that the person has no long-term interest in the company. Participants in this study were asked to give the average number of times in a year that they went out of town to visit relatives.

Cultural Values as Factors

Cultural values unique to Appalachians have often been cited as factors making transition to urban areas difficult and limiting occupational attainments. Appalachians are said to be independent (Ergood,1976), and a spirit of independence makes it difficult to take orders or follow instructions from a supervisor. If workers fail to follow instructions, then they can expect to be overlooked when promotions are available. Independence was measured by a four-item scale in which persons indicated how often they broke rules at work to do a job the way they thought best, got mad at a person in authority, argued with a person in authority, or did what they were told even if they did not like it. The sum of these responses produced a scale with a reliability of .65.

Appalachians are said not to trust institutions (Ergood, 1976). Institutions are characteristic of workplaces in cities. They are formalized, large, structured places where an individual may know and be known by only a handful of the total people who work there. Confidence in institutions was measured by the amount of confidence people reported in six different institutions common to urban areas. The sum of these responses produced a scale with a reliability of .84.

Appalachians are said to be traditionalistic (Ergood, 1976). Traditionalism makes it difficult to change and change is necessary to adapt from a rural area to an urban place. Traditionalism was measured by a four-item scale in which people reported their perceptions of society; the reliability of the scale was .79.

Appalachians are said to be fatalistic. Fatalism implies an acceptance of the world the way it is because one feels there is nothing which can be done to make things better by one's own efforts. A fatalistic person would not attempt to get ahead because the person would not see that such efforts would have any connection with eventual outcomes. Fatalism was measured by a two-item scale with a reliability of .42.

Appalachians also are said to maintain a pattern of moving back and forth between Appalachia and the place where they migrate. Stereotypically, they are said to move to the city, where they accumulate a little money, and then go back to Appalachia and stay until it runs out. If this is so, it would make it difficult to achieve success in an urban occupation because no seniority would be built up and an employer would be reluctant to promote a worker who is expected to leave after a short time. Participants in this study were asked whether they had ever moved away from the Cincinnati area since first living there.

The relative effects of these variables on the occupational attainments of Appalachians can be seen by the standardized regression coefficients in Table 5.5. The most important variables influencing occupational attainments are the background factors of educational attainment, family of origin, and the size of the place where an individual grew up. The most important of these is education, which has an effect more than three times as great as the next most

TABLE 5.5
Relative Effects of Determinants of Job
Attainments among Appalachians
(standardized regression coefficients)

Predictor Variable	β
Background	
Education	.58
Father's occupation	.16
Size place raised	.11
Family interaction	
Frequency of out-of-town visits	−.03
Came to Cincinnati because family there	−.17
Found job through family	−.15
Values	
Submission to authority	.003
Confidence in institutions	−.08
Traditionalism	.08
Fatalism	−.04
Moved away from Cincinnati	−.10

important variable. Independent of an individual's ability or of any other factor, educational attainment is a necessary prerequisite to obtaining most jobs in urban areas. Unlike small towns, where employers have known potential workers most of their lives, companies in urban areas frequently delegate hiring to personnel departments, where individuals fill out forms and, on the basis of the information they provide, are either screened out or called for an interview. If individuals indicate they do not have adequate years of education, employers take that as an indication of either low intelligence or undependability. For all groups, including Appalachians, education is a major factor, if not the major factor, in determining the level of occupation an individual may be able to obtain.

The Background Factor

Family background is also an important factor in the occupational attainment process among Appalachian migrants. The higher the occupational status of the family in which the migrant was raised, the higher the occupational status the Appalachian will be able to achieve in the urban environment. Schwarzweller et al. (1971) noted, in their study of migrants from Beech Creek, that those migrants who came from higher-status families did better than those from poorer families. These findings would appear to be applicable not only to migrants from Beech Creek, but to Appalachians in general. Middle-class families provide benefits to children beyond their ability to secure more years of education. They give them aspirations which are higher than those of the children of lower-status families (Sewell, 1972). The higher the goals the individual holds, the higher the ultimate level of achievement will be. They socialize them in skills which are more beneficial in performing higher-status jobs than are the values which children in working-class families obtain (Kohn, 1969). The middle-class child is better able to make a presentation of self to a potential employer and thereby acquire a better job than a working-class child with the same amount of education.

A rural background continues to be a disadvantage in the occupational attainment process among urban Appalachians. The larger the place where the Appalachian was raised, the higher the occupational achievement. Appalachians who moved to Cincinnati from a farm or small town have more of an adjustment to make than does an individual raised in a metropolitan area. Not only must they expend energies in obtaining and performing an occupational role; they must also adjust to differences in school systems, differences in housing, differences in city services, differences in shopping for even ordinary things like groceries, differences in recreation, and numerous rules and regulations essential for cities but nonexistent in smaller places. Persons raised in metropolitan areas learn to do these things while growing up — in fact, they never learn to do them any other way. A migrant from a smaller place has to learn to do these things while at the same time performing an occupational role as an adult.

Dependence upon family hinders the occupational attainments of Appalachians. The frequent visits which Appalachians are said to make back home are not important. Whether the migrant goes out of town to visit relatives every week, or not at all, makes no difference in the level of attainment at work. However, choosing to come to Cincinnati because relatives were already there, and obtaining a job with their help, do reduce the level of occupational achievement. Appalachians who came to Cincinnati because relatives were there have lower-status jobs than Appalachians who chose Cincinnati for some other reason, and Appalachians who found jobs without the help of their families have better jobs than those whose dependence upon family was greater. How common this dependence is, and whether it is more common among Appalachians than among other groups, remain to be seen.

As previously noted, families are limited in the assistance they can provide relatives. It seems certain that they cannot obtain jobs for relatives which are better than the jobs they themselves have. This sets a ceiling upon the job attainments of persons who depend upon family to help them find work. Persons who secure jobs without help from relatives have a broader range of possibilities. Some of these people will get better jobs than those of their relatives and this will increase the average occupational attainments of these people.

Adherence to values, said to be common among Appalachians, has no effect upon the occupational attainment of individuals. An individual who is independent, traditionalistic, fatalistic, and is reluctant to trust institutions does as well occupationally as a person who is at the opposite end on any or all of these criteria. The standardized regression coefficients associated with all of these variables are less than .10. Whether or not Appalachians living in urban areas subscribe to these values remains to be seen, but the important fact is that these values are not relevant to the occupational attainment process. They may or may not be Appalachian characteristics, but they do not explain why Appalachians have lower occupational attainments than do other groups.

Appalachians who have moved away from Cincinnati, and then back, pay the price of lower occupational attainments in Cincinnati. If Appalachians do return to Appalachia whenever they accumulate a little money, or even if they return to Appalachia when laid off from work, they forego opportunities in Cincinnati. A person who stays in Cincinnati and looks for new work will do better than those who go back to Appalachia and wait until relatives find them a new job. A person who quits a job loses seniority and related promotional opportunities. Movement away from Cincinnati and then back is not a major explanation for the lower occupational attainments of Appalachians, but it does have a negative effect.

Table 5.6 shows how Appalachians compare to other groups on those variables related to occupational achievement. In terms of those background factors

TABLE 5.6
Means of Determinants of Job Attainment

Predictor Variable	White Appalachian Migrant	Other White Migrant	Black	White Cincinnati Native
Background				
Education	10.81	12.98*	10.71	12.61*
Father's occupation	22.92	42.35*	21.18	42.31*
Size of place one was raised in	1.59	2.30*	2.22*	3.00*
Family interaction				
Frequency of visits	4.09	4.18	2.27*	1.66*
Came because of family	0.12	0.19	0.27*	0.00*
Found job through family	0.30	0.22	0.31	0.41
Values				
Submission to authority	12.49	11.28*	12.40	11.75
Confidence in institutions	7.19	6.84	7.35	6.92
Traditionalism	5.43	4.00*	5.52	4.66*
Fatalism	1.48	1.59	2.06*	1.67
Moved away from Cincinnati	0.25	0.27	0.20	0.21
Occupational SEI score	32.36	50.46*	30.30*	44.23*

*Significantly different from means for white Appalachian migrants ($p < .05$).

which are the key to occupational achievement, Appalachians fare poorly compared to white migrants from other areas and to white natives in Cincinnati and are approximately equal to blacks. The average education of Appalachians is 10.81 years, which is about the same as for blacks (10.71 years), but much lower than for either white migrants from other areas (12.98 years) or white natives (12.61 years). If educational attainment is the primary factor on which occupational selection is based, Appalachians are clearly at a disadvantage in competing with other white groups. The difference is even more than the two years would indicate, for the average Appalachian has less than a high school education, while other whites average a high school degree and a little more.

The families of origin from which Appalachians come are of much lower status than the families of other white migrants or natives of Cincinnati. The average SEI score of the fathers of Appalachians in Cincinnati is only 22.92, compared to 42.35 for other white migrants and 42.31 for natives of Cincinnati. This difference reflects a severe limitation in the relative resources which Appalachians' families were able to provide them in their youth. Not only were they less able to help them secure an education, but they were less able to socialize them in the middle-class ways which often determine success or failure in the attainment of better jobs.

Appalachians were, on the average, raised in smaller places than were people in any of the other groups. Appalachians were more likely to be raised on farms or in small towns, while white migrants from other areas and blacks moved to Cincinnati from another metropolitan area. Consequently, the adjustments which Appalachians must make are greater than the adjustments of other groups.

Appalachians compete unfavorably with other white migrants and natives in Cincinnati for jobs which are available, at least in part because of major disadvantages in educational attainment, family backgrounds, and places raised.

While dependency upon family has been shown to reduce the occupational attainments of those Appalachians who are so dependent, Appalachians are not more dependent upon their families than are people from other groups. Only 12 percent of those Appalachians who migrated to Cincinnati indicated that they came because other family members were there. This is lower than the percentage of other white migrants who came because of family (19 percent) and less than half the percentage of blacks who came for family reasons (27 percent). The percentage of white migrants from other areas who depended upon their families to help them find jobs is lower than that of Appalachians — 22 percent and 30 percent, respectively; but the same percentage of blacks and a higher percentage of natives in Cincinnati were dependent upon their families. While dependency upon family is a factor which reduces the level of occupation individuals reach, Appalachians are not more dependent, and may even be slightly less dependent, than are members of other groups. The amount that Appalachians depend upon their families for assistance in adjusting to Cincinnati and finding jobs does not explain why their occupational attainments are lower than those of other white migrants or natives of Cincinnati.

Appalachians do go out of town more often than blacks or natives of Cincinnati, to visit relatives. They and other white migrants both average slightly more than four trips a year. But, frequency of out-of-town visits was not found to be a factor in the occupational attainment process.

Although Appalachians are said to value independence, traditionalism, fatalism, and have little trust in institutions, on only one of these variables did Appalachians rank higher than other groups. The findings do indicate that Appalachians are more traditionalistic than are members of other white groups, both migrants and natives, and about equal to the traditionalism of blacks. In terms of independence, Appalachians were found to be the most submissive to authority. White migrants from other areas and natives of Cincinnati were found to be much more independent and less submissive. This may well be a result of the relative occupational attainments of the different groups. Independence is necessary to the successful performance of professional and managerial work, while submission to authority is necessary for blue-collar workers (Kohn, 1969). Since Appalachians are most often blue-collar workers, while other whites are professionals or managers, it is reasonable that independence would be more common among these groups, and not Appalachians.

Contrary to popular opinion, Appalachians and blacks had more confidence in institutions than did either white migrants from other areas or natives of Cincinnati. It is not known why this is so. It could be due to a sampling error or it could be that other groups are more cautious. In any event, there is no support for the statement that Appalachians are more distrustful of institutions in urban areas.

Appalachians are found to be the least fatalistic of any group. They are very similar in this belief to white migrants from other areas and to natives of Cincinnati and less fatalistic than are blacks. This means that they are the most likely to believe that they have the ability to influence their own outcomes. There is perhaps a selectivity function involved here. Persons who choose to migrate obviously believe that they are doing something which will make their lives better. It may be that the fatalistic Appalachians stayed in Appalachia and the efficacious ones moved. In any case, Appalachians in urban areas are not more fatalistic than are other people.

Not only are those values which are ascribed to Appalachians unrelated to occupational achievement, but they aren't even unique to Appalachian people. In fact, other groups with higher occupational achievements are more likely to hold these values than Appalachians are. These values in no way appear to account for the lower occupational attainments among Appalachians.

Appalachians have moved away from Cincinnati and back with approximately the same frequency as white migrants from other places: 25 percent and 27 percent of these groups, respectively, have left and returned, while 20 percent of blacks and 21 percent of Cincinnati natives have done so. It would appear that such movement is common to people in all groups.

The only major differences between Appalachians and others on those variables related to occupational attainment are in the background variables of educational attainment, family background, and place of origin. On those variables, Appalachians are at a serious disadvantage compared to either white migrants from other places or natives of Cincinnati. On other variables, Appalachians compare favorably. They are not more dependent upon their families, they do not subscribe more frequently to values which have been held to limit occupational attainments, and they do not leave Cincinnati and return more often than do other groups.

Not only are the backgrounds of Appalachians different from those of people of other groups, but their backgrounds appear to be a greater factor in the occupational attainment process. Table 5.7 indicates that Appalachians acquire an additional 4.74 SEI points for each year of education, which is almost three times the importance of education for other white migrants and about twice the importance education has for white natives. The importance of education is similar for Appalachians and blacks. Family background has about twice the effect among Appalachians as it does among either blacks or white natives

TABLE 5.7
Comparative Effects of Determinants of Job Attainment (unstandardized regression coefficients)

Predictor Variable	White Appalachian Migrant	Other White Migrant	Black	White Cincinnati Native
Background				
Education	4.74	1.70	4.99	2.89
Father's occupation	0.19	0.24	−0.07	0.09
Size of place where one was raised	2.05	0.10	−1.84	—[a]
Family interaction				
Frequency of visits	−0.12	0.44	−0.72	0.81
Came because of family	−12.37	−7.44	0.82	—[a]
Found job through family	−7.84	−2.16	0.85	−8.07
Values				
Submission to authority	0.03	−0.21	−0.42	0.98
Confidence in institutions	−0.76	−0.25	0.70	−0.33
Traditionalism	0.59	−1.33	1.64	0.07
Fatalism	−0.70	−0.23	0.97	1.47
Moved away from Cincinnati	−5.08	0.74	−5.48	1.12
Intercept	−17.76	27.74	−26.66	−6.32

[a]Coefficient is not given because variable is a constant.

of Cincinnati and about the same effect as it does among other white migrants. Size of the place of origin is more important to Appalachians than to either of the other three groups.

These findings indicate that backgrounds are a more serious liability for Appalachians than for people in other groups. Educational attainment matters less to other white migrants or natives of Cincinnati. This means that if a person in one of those groups fails to acquire enough years of education, that person has a better chance at a good job than does an Appalachian with the same educational attainment. Not only are the educational attainments of Appalachians low, but the failure to acquire an education affects them more seriously than other people. The same is true for the father's occupation. The achievement of blacks and natives of Cincinnati is largely unaffected by the occupational attainments of their fathers. Appalachians and other white migrants both receive better jobs if their fathers held better jobs, independent of years of education or of other variables. However, because the fathers of Appalachians typically held low-status jobs, while the fathers of other white migrants held above-average jobs, this means that, on the whole, other white migrants benefit from the above-average jobs their fathers held, while Appalachians suffer from the low-status attainments of their fathers. Rural backgrounds continue to further lower the level of attainments of Appalachians who have migrated. Those who were raised in the city appear to be doing better, but since rural backgrounds are common among Appalachians, the typical migrant is hindered in the occupational attainment process. If these findings are valid, they indicate that qualifications are more stringent for an Appalachian or a black than for either a white native or a migrant from someplace else. One of the latter might be able to get a good job, with lower qualifications, than an Appalachian or a black could. It seems to take more to be a qualified Appalachian or a qualified black.

Dependency upon family also appears to be a greater liability among Appalachians than among other groups. Appalachians who came to Cincinnati because their families were there have an average occupation showing 12.37 fewer SEI points than do Appalachians who came to Cincinnati for other reasons, and those who found a job through help from their families have occupations showing 7.84 fewer SEI points. Obtaining a job through family connections is as serious for natives of Cincinnati but much less serious for other white migrants and even a slight asset for blacks. While Appalachians are not more dependent upon their families than are people in other groups, those who are suffer more.

Those values which are ascribed to Appalachians and sometimes put forth as an explanation for their lack of occupational success have already been shown to have little effect upon Appalachians and to be not stronger among Appalachians than among other groups. Table 5.7 indicates that none of those values is important to the occupational success of any group. Those theories which rest upon cultural conflict appear to receive no support as far as their effects upon occupational achievement are concerned. Background and family relationships are much more important.

Finally, movement away from Cincinnati reduces the occupational achievement of Appalachians and blacks, while it slightly increases the achievements of other whites. Perhaps a difference occurs in the reasons for migration. Other white migrants and natives of Cincinnati may leave the area to attend universities in other cities and may return when their education is complete. As a result, those who have been away do better than those who stayed. Appalachians and blacks who leave Cincinnati perhaps more often go back to the places they originally came from. As a result, they forego opportunities in Cincinnati while doing little to improve their marketability at the time of their return.

These findings demonstrate that Appalachians not only rank lower on those variables which assist occupational attainment, but are hindered more by a lack of those resources than are people in other groups. On the whole, they suffer more if they lack an adequate education, come from a low-status family, are raised in rural areas, depend upon their families, or move away from Cincinnati. The same variables which account for occupational achievements in the general population are also responsible for the occupational allocation among Appalachians, but they affect Appalachians more than they affect other people. A black, a white native of Cincinnati, or a migrant who came from someplace else has a better chance of overcoming a disadvantaged position on one of these variables than an Appalachian does.

The importance of the observed differences in factors in the occupational attainment process and differences in the effects those variables create in that process are estimated, as was the case with income attainment, by replacing the averages of one group with the unstandardized regression coefficients of another group. The effects that differences in levels of these variables and in effects these variables have on Appalachians are shown in Table 5.8.

If Appalachians had the resources of either other white migrants or natives of the Cincinnati area, they would have higher occupational attainments than

TABLE 5.8
Predicted Job Attainments of Appalachians, Based upon Levels of Resources and Efficacy of Resources Found in Reference Groups

	Predicted Job Attainments of Appalachians	
Reference Group	*Appalachian efficacy; Reference-Group Resources*	*Appalachian resources; Reference-Group Efficacy*
Appalachians	32.36	32.36
Other white migrants	46.99	40.24
Blacks	31.12	28.93
Natives	48.39	40.54

they presently have. The greater educational attainment among these groups is the major factor responsible for the gain which Appalachians would consequently receive. The only other factor where there is much of a difference is in family background. In short, those variables which are the most important in the occupational attainment process are where the greatest differences exist between Appalachians and other groups. If Appalachians had the same family backgrounds and education as white migrants from other areas, they could expect to have occupations 15 SEI points higher than they presently average. It would appear that the typical Appalachian migrant is poorly educated and from a low-status family, while the migrant who comes to Cincinnati from other places is well educated and from a middle-class family. As a result of these differences, a major difference occurs in the level of occupations they reach in the Cincinnati area.

Appalachians would have approximately the same occupational attainments as they now have if they had the same resources as blacks. This again demonstrates the similarity between blacks and Appalachians in the Cincinnati area. In terms of education and family background, they are almost identical. Appalachians have more often migrated from rural areas, but blacks have more often come to Cincinnati because of family connections. These differences largely cancel each other out.

Appalachians pay a higher price for limited backgrounds than do members of other white groups. The second column of Table 5.8 shows that if Appalachians were rewarded for what they had in the same way as are other white migrants, they could expect an average occupation with an SEI score of 40.24, and if they were rewarded in the same way as are Cincinnati natives, their average SEI score would be 40.54. Instead, it is 32.36. They would only do worse if they were rewarded the way blacks seem to be.

Again this seems to indicate that Appalachians who have a good education, come from middle-class families, and are raised in larger cities compete well with people in other groups who have similar resources. But Appalachians who do not have these advantages pay a higher price than either other white migrants or Cincinnati natives. For example, removing the effects of other variables, if a person has a college education (16 years) and comes from a middle-class family (SEI score of 75) in an urban area, that person, if an Appalachian, can expect to obtain an occupation with an SEI score of 55.44, and, if another white migrant, 63.89. However, if the person has only an eighth-grade education and comes from a rural area and a family with low occupational attainment (SEI score of 25), that person, if an Appalachian, can expect an occupation with an SEI score of 16.18, but, if another white migrant, 37.60. The disadvantage for Appalachians with limited backgrounds is more than three times the disadvantage for those who have secured a college education and are fortunate enough to come from middle-class homes in urban areas. Those college-educated Appalachians from middle-class homes and urban areas do almost as well as other whites, but the majority of Appalachians do not have these assets. As a result, they appear to be deprived of jobs which are given instead to Cincinnati natives and other white migrants with similar credentials.

Three major conclusions are produced by this analysis of differences in the occupational attainment processes of Appalachians and other groups. First, Appalachians are at a disadvantage in the competition for available jobs because of limitations in their backgrounds. They have less education, come from lower-status families, and are more often raised in rural areas. These disadvantages make it difficult to compete with other whites who are better educated, from middle-class families, and more often raised in cities. The disadvantages of Appalachians are at approximately the same level as those found among blacks.

Second, these disadvantages have more serious consequences for Appalachians than for other white groups. A white migrant who came to Cincinnati from someplace other than Appalachia or a white native of Cincinnati, if that person lacks advantages provided by education and family background, suffers less than an Appalachian. Appalachians who acquire a good education and come from middle-class families compete favorably with other people for jobs in Cincinnati, but few Appalachians have these advantages. When Appalachians with relatively few years of education, who were raised in working-class families, compete with other whites with the same lack of education and the same family backgrounds, the better jobs go to the other whites, and not to Appalachians. Disadvantages in education and family background have even more serious consequences for blacks. This accounts for the fact that other whites who are blue-collar workers are most often employed in skilled trades while Appalachians are left semiskilled and unskilled positions. Blacks are more often found in the lowest unskilled jobs. This would seem to imply that if an employer has a choice, other things being equal, white natives of Cincinnati and other white migrants are hired first, then Appalachians are hired, and the last jobs go to blacks. When jobs run out, the blacks are left unemployed.

Third, these findings indicate that characteristics ascribed to Appalachians and often set forth as explanations for their lack of occupational success are neither unique among Appalachians nor very important in the occupational attainment process. Dependence upon family did lower levels of occupational achievement, but Appalachians were not more dependent upon families than were other groups. Values ascribed as part of Appalachian culture were shown to be neither uniquely identified with Appalachians nor important to occupational attainment. Explanations based upon cultural conflict appear unnecessary in understanding the relatively low occupational attainments of Appalachians.

EDUCATIONAL ATTAINMENT

The previous discussion identified education as the most important variable determining the occupational attainments of Appalachians. It was shown to be more than three times as important as the second most important variable.

Appalachians were also shown to have lower-than-average levels of education — two years less than the average education of white Cincinnati natives and white migrants from places other than Appalachia. This inequality in educational attainment was shown in Chapter 4 to be present in both the first- and the second-generation migrants. The purpose here is to understand the process of educational attainment among Appalachians and how that process differs from the educational attainment process among other groups.

Family background has been identified as one of the most important variables determining educational attainment in the general population. Individuals who are raised in middle-class families are generally placed in better school systems, given greater encouragement by their parents, and provided resources not available to working- and lower-class children. In this study, family background is, again, indicated by the occupation the individual's father held while the person was growing up.

A second background factor included in the analysis is size of the place where one is raised. A person raised in the city may grow up realizing that few opportunities are available to the uneducated. City schools are often geared to college preparatory programs where college attendance is expected.

Some have held that Appalachians do not realize the importance of education and therefore more readily drop out. The perception of the importance of education was determined in two different ways. First, those persons who had less than a high school education were asked if they felt they needed more education than they had obtained. Responses were categorized as simply yes or no. Second, all individuals were asked to estimate the percentage of adult Americans who are college graduates. If a person perceives that a high percentage of persons are college graduates, then that person may also perceive that failure to obtain a college education makes one unable to compete in the job market. The lower the percentage of college graduates perceived, the less necessary a college education becomes as perceived.

Finally, values which are held to be part of Appalachian culture could influence the amount of education obtained. Submission to authority, confidence in institutions, traditionalism, and fatalism were measured, as in the previous discussion, and entered into the educational attainment model studied here.

Table 5.9 shows the relative importance of each of these factors in the educational attainment process of Appalachians living in the Cincinnati area. The most important variable appears to be the value of traditionalism. The more traditionalistic the Appalachian is, the fewer the years of education obtained. Traditionalism reflects the belief that old ways are best. It involves a glorification of the past. Individuals who subscribe to those values, and who come from families which had few years of education, drop out of school earlier than other persons. They may well believe that their parents made out all right without an education, so they can too. They may react negatively to conflicts between what the educational system is teaching and beliefs they have traditionally held.

TABLE 5.9
Relative Effects of Determinants of Educational Attainment among Appalachians
(standardized regression coefficients)

Predictor Variable	β
Background	
Father's occupation	.32
Size of place one was raised in	.11
Importance of education	
More education believed needed	.07
Estimate of college graduates	−.18
Values	
Submission to authority	.08
Confidence in institutions	−.01
Traditionalism	−.42
Fatalism	−.02

It is also possible that values change as an individual obtains more years of education. College students are notorious for the conflicts they experience between the values their parents taught and the values they see in their peers. It is therefore possible that those Appalachians who obtained more years of education have become less traditionalistic, while those who left the educational system earlier have not. It is not possible to clearly say whether a traditionalistic person has fewer years of education, or whether a person is more traditionalistic because of having fewer years of education. All that is clear is that adherence to the value of traditionalism is linked to fewer years of education. None of the other values supposedly identified with Appalachian culture — submission to authority, confidence in institutions, or fatalism — was related to educational attainment.

Family background is the second most important variable determining the years of education an Appalachian received. The higher the occupational status of the Appalachian's father, the more years of education the person obtained. Parents who hold higher-status jobs realize the importance of education in their own attainments and therefore stress the importance of education to their children, divert resources for the education of their children, and often consider educational attainment less a matter of choice and more a requirement. Family background is an important variable in the educational attainment process of Appalachians as well as among the general population.

The size of the place where one was raised also has an impact on educational attainment among Appalachians, although not as much as family background or traditionalism. The larger the place where an Appalachian grew up, the more years of education obtained. In rural areas and small towns, educational attainment is less common. Few jobs require a college education and many are obtained by persons with fewer than elementary school years. Rural schools often ended at the fourth grade a few years ago and seldom went beyond the eighth. In order to obtain even a high school education, it was necessary to ride a bus into a nearby town. A child growing up in such an area seldom encountered role models who had much education and, if the child was even to graduate from high school, it was often logistically not easy to do so.

The only other variable related to educational attainment was the estimated percentage of college graduates in the population. The fewer years of education a person had, the higher the percentage of college graduates the person perceived. For some years, Fox and Philliber (1975, 1977) have studied the relationship between socioeconomic status and perceptions of affluence. In general, they have found that the lower the socioeconomic status of an individual, the greater the amount of affluence perceived in others. Perception of the presence of college graduates is more likely a consequence of educational attainment than a cause.

In the previous discussion, we observed how the backgrounds and values of Appalachians differed from those of other groups. The families in which Appalachians were raised were of lower socioeconomic status than the families of other whites and were similar to those of blacks. Appalachians were also more frequently raised in small towns and rural areas. Since both of these variables were related to educational attainments among Appalachians, it is possible that they have less education than either other white migrants or natives of Cincinnati because of limitations in their backgrounds.

Few differences existed in the value systems of Appalachians and other groups. However, Appalachians and blacks were found to be more traditionalistic than either white migrants from other areas or natives of Cincinnati, and traditionalism is related to educational attainments among Appalachians. It is possible that Appalachians and blacks have less education because they are more traditionalistic in their outlook.

In Table 5.10, group differences in the importance of education are presented, along with the other variables used to predict educational attainment. What these data demonstrate is that Appalachians do not value education less than do members of other white groups: 67 percent of the Appalachians who had less than a high school education felt they needed more than they had. This is almost identical to the 68 percent of white migrants from other places who felt it, and higher than the 55 percent of white Cincinnati natives. Only blacks, among whom 89 percent of school dropouts felt a need for more education, were more likely to believe they needed more education. Appalachians were also similar to other white groups in their estimation of the percentage of college graduates in the population but lower in their estimation than blacks. To the extent these two measures indicate the importance of education, it must be concluded that Appalachians perceive the value of education as much as do other

TABLE 5.10
Means of Determinants of Educational Attainment

Predictor Variable	White Appalachian Migrant	Other White Migrant	Black	White Cincinnati Native
Background				
Father's occupation	22.92	42.35*	21.18	42.31*
Size of place one was				
raised in	1.59	2.30*	2.22*	3.00*
Importance of education				
More education believed				
needed	0.67	0.68	0.89*	0.55
Estimate of college				
graduates	30.59	31.57	40.99*	31.36
Values				
Submission to authority	12.49	11.28*	12.40	11.75
Confidence in institutions	7.19	6.84	7.36	6.92
Traditionalism	5.43	4.00*	5.52	4.66*
Fatalism	1.48	1.59	2.06*	1.67
Education	10.81	12.98*	10.71	12.61*

*Significantly different from means for white Appalachian migrants (p $<$.05).

white groups and less than blacks. The fact that other white groups have greater average educational attainments cannot be due to their greater recognition of the importance of education.

The process of educational attainment appears to be more similar among Appalachians and other groups than was the process by which occupations were obtained. Table 5.11 shows the effects that each of the predictor variables has among each of the reference groups. The effect of family background, indicated by the father's occupation, is identical among Appalachians and other white migrants and only slightly greater than the importance of family background among white Cincinnati natives. In each of these groups, the higher the socio-economic status of the family in which the individual was raised, the greater the number of years of education obtained. Among blacks, the effect of family background is less, reflecting the greater mobility which we previously observed. Black socioeconomic status has changed sufficiently within the last few years to lessen the negative impact of low socioeconomic origins. However, the origins of blacks were so low that they have not made up the difference between their educational attainments and those of other groups.

The size of the place where a person was raised is a factor in the educational attainment process of Appalachians and blacks, but not in that of other white migrants. Appalachians, and especially blacks, obtained fewer years of education if they came from small towns and farms. Blacks who grew up in rural areas may not have had an opportunity to obtain an education. Many of these people grew up when dual school systems were legal, and that meant that schools for blacks did not always exist. As a result, blacks living in those areas obtained few years of formal education. Why a rural background should be a hindrance to Appalachians, but not other white migrants, is a mystery. The data clearly indicate this is so. Other white migrants from small towns and rural areas obtain even slightly more education than those from cities. The same effect was observed in the process of occupational attainment, independent of education. Appalachian migration is clearly not simply rural-to-urban migration. Not all Appalachians come from rural areas and those who did are affected differently by the experience than are migrants from other areas.

The effect of the perception of the importance of education is almost identical for Appalachians and other white migrants, but a difference does exist among blacks and white Cincinnati natives. White Cincinnati natives who perceived they needed more education had an average of 0.89 years more education than those who did not perceive they needed more education. Among

TABLE 5.11

Comparative Effects of Determinants of Educational Attainment (unstandardized regression coefficients)

Predictor Variable	White Appalachian Migrant	Other White Migrant	Black	White Cincinnati Native
Background				
Father's occupation	0.04	0.04	0.02	0.03
Size of place one was raised in	0.24	−0.04	1.07	−[a]
Importance of education				
More education believed needed	0.40	0.36	−1.75	0.89
Estimate of college graduates	−0.03	−0.04	−0.01	−0.02
Values				
Submission to authority	0.08	−0.18	−0.06	0.03
Confidence in institutions	−0.01	−0.10	−0.05	−0.23
Traditionalism	−0.39	−0.37	−0.25	−0.25
Fatalism	−0.05	0.05	0.13	−0.11
Intercept	11.22	16.53	12.08	13.89

[a]Coefficient is not given because variable is a constant.

Cincinnati natives, but not among either Appalachians or other white migrants, there is support for the observation that those who obtained few years of education did so because they failed to recognize its importance. Among blacks, the pattern is reversed. Those who perceived they needed more education averaged 1.75 fewer years of education. This is consistent with the earlier interpretation: that blacks average fewer years of education not because they fail to recognize its importance, but because they have not had an adequate opportunity.

The only value which is consistently related to educational attainment is traditionalism. Among all four groups, the more traditionalistic the individual, the fewer years of education obtained. The effect, however, is stronger among Appalachians and among other white migrants than among blacks and white Cincinnati natives. Traditionalism is found to be more common among Appalachians than among other groups and to be a greater limitation on educational attainment. The glorification of the past, which traditionalism implies, may not have the same meaning for Appalachians as it does for blacks or Cincinnati natives. The past for Cincinnati natives is in Cincinnati, where there exists an urban occupational and educational system. In the past, and in the present, individuals were expected to obtain a formal education. What blacks value in their past may not be related in their minds to a lack of education. Although traditionalism is as common among blacks as among Appalachians, blacks are the most likely to believe that education is needed. As a result, traditionalism limits the educational attainment of Appalachians more than it does for blacks or white Cincinnati natives.

Table 5.12 shows that differences in resources and their consequences affect educational attainment in much the same way they affected income and occupational attainments. Appalachians have fewer resources than other white groups and the lack of those resources costs an Appalachian more than it costs another white. The first column of figures shows how the educational

TABLE 5.12
Predicted Educational Attainments of Appalachians, Based upon Levels of Resources and Efficacy of Resources Found in Reference Groups

	Predicted Education of Appalachians	
	---	---
Reference Group	Appalachian efficacy; Reference-Group Resources	Appalachian resources; Reference-Group Efficacy
Appalachians	10.81	10.81
Other white migrants	11.97	11.50
Blacks	10.40	10.48
Natives	11.88	11.77

attainments of Appalachians would change if they had the resources of other groups. They would average an additional year of education if they had the resources found among either other white migrants or white Cincinnati natives. The major reasons for this are the differences in family background and in traditionalism. Lower socioeconomic origins and greater traditionalism lower the educational attainments of Appalachians by almost half a year each, compared to the attainments of other white groups. The other factors contribute little to the difference.

There are few differences in the resources of blacks and Appalachians and, as a result, it would not make much difference if Appalachians had the average resources of blacks. However, consistent with the pattern of income and occupational attainments, Appalachians would average lower educational attainments if they had the average resources of blacks. The difference, however, is less than half a year.

The second column of figures shows how the educational attainments of Appalachians would change if they converted their resources into years of education at the same rate as do other groups. Again Appalachians would have more years of education if their payoffs for resources were the same as those for other white migrants or natives, and fewer years of education if their payoffs were like those for blacks. The data in Table 5.11 demonstrate that an Appalachian with fewer resources, particularly coming from a rural area and showing greater traditionalism, pays a higher price in educational attainment than do other whites. For example, removing the effects of other differences, a person from an urban area who is nontraditionalistic, if an Appalachian, could expect 13.27 years of education, and, if another white migrant, 14.43 years, a difference of slightly more than a year. That same person, if from a rural area, traditionalistic, and a white migrant from outside Appalachia, can expect 10.11 years of education, but, if an Appalachian, only 7.87 years, a difference of 2.24 years. A Cincinnati native who is nontraditionalistic can expect 13.77 years of education, compared to 12.93 for an Appalachian, while a traditionalistic Cincinnati native can expect 10.77 years of education, compared to 8.25 for an Appalachian. Coming from a rural area with traditionalistic values doubles the difference between Appalachians and other white migrants, and having traditionalistic values triples the difference between Appalachians and Cincinnati natives.

To some extent, differences in the educational attainments of Appalachians and other white groups may be expected to diminish over time as a higher percentage of Appalachians are born in the urban areas where their parents migrated. These findings demonstrate that Appalachians are less likely to have been raised in urban areas and pay a higher price than other groups because of that. However, findings presented earlier in this study, which are consistent with other studies (Maloney, 1974; Wagner, 1978), indicate that the children of Appalachian migrants have serious problems succeeding in urban schools and frequently drop out before completion.

This system is self-perpetuating from one generation to the next. If a person from a lower-socioeconomic-status home leaves school before graduation, the only job available to that person is one which has low socioeconomic status. In turn, the children of that person will obtain fewer average years of education and be qualified only for a lower-socioeconomic-status job. Recognizing this system of self-perpetuation among blacks, society has intervened in the process and, as a result, the average educational and occupational attainments of blacks have substantially improved, although they remain below other groups. A similar effort may be necessary to increase educational attainments among Appalachians.

There is some indication that at least one Appalachian cultural value is partly responsible for the failure to obtain enough years of education: Appalachians who valued traditionalism obtained fewer years of education than did others. Adherence to traditionalism was also related to lower educational attainments among other groups, but its effect was stronger among Appalachians and other white migrants than among blacks or white Cincinnati natives. Traditionalism was also more common among Appalachians and blacks than among other white groups. It is not possible to say whether Appalachians have less education because of greater traditionalism, or show greater traditionalism because they have less education. It is most likely that Appalachian parents, who have low educational attainments, teach their children the value of traditionalism, and that the acceptance of that value reduces the probability of higher educational attainments in the second generation.

SUMMARY

These findings show evidence of the uniqueness of Appalachians in Cincinnati. They do not have lower-status jobs and lower family incomes merely because of limited backgrounds. Those factors are important, but equally important are differences in the attainment processes for education, occupations, and income. There has been speculation that Appalachian family structure and cultural values have hindered Appalachians in their competition for jobs and wages. However, these data indicate that what are supposedly Appalachian family structures and cultural values are neither particularly unique to Appalachians or relevant in the competition for jobs and wages. There is no evidence that Appalachians have brought with them a culture that is unadaptable to the urban environment. Appalachians are affected in the attainment of education, occupation, and income by the same variables which affect other groups, but they are affected differently.

Appalachians have fewer resources than either Cincinnati natives or white migrants from other places, and those fewer resources do result in lower educational, occupational, and income attainments. Appalachians come from families of lower socioeconomic status, living in rural areas, and place a greater value on traditionalism — all of which results in fewer years of educational attainment. Fewer years of education, combined with lower family origins and rural backgrounds, in turn result in lower occupational attainments. Finally, lower occupational and educational attainments, plus the fact that wives are less likely to participate in the labor force, result in lower family income.

Fewer resources only partially account for the lower attainments of Appalachians. Equally important is the fact that Appalachians without those resources pay a higher price than other whites, whether natives or migrants. Many people have come from rural areas, with an emphasis on traditionalism, to live in Cincinnati, but an Appalachian with those characteristics is at a greater disadvantage than either Cincinnati natives or other white migrants. Similarly, the failure to obtain enough years of education, to come from a middle-class family, or to have been raised in an urban area has greater consequences for the jobs that Appalachians obtain. The failure to obtain an education also has a greater effect upon the income which Appalachians earn.

A white migrant from some other area or a Cincinnati native who comes from a lower family background, lacks enough years of education, or was raised on a farm still has a chance of obtaining a good job and earning a good income, but an Appalachian must have these resources to expect to compete. Appalachians with middle-class backgrounds, especially those who migrated to Cincinnati from cities within Appalachia, appear to assimilate well into the competition for education, occupation, and income in Cincinnati. They obtain almost as much education as other white groups and, once they do, can expect jobs and wages equal to those of other whites. The probability is high that many of these people pass without being recognized as Appalachians. The problem arises for those Appalachians who are not so endowed, and they are the majority. They are less likely than other whites with similar backgrounds to obtain as much education, to obtain as good a job, or to receive as good an income. The socioeconomic structure appears to accept Appalachians on equal terms with other whites if, but only if, they come educated and from middle-class origins.

6

MORE THAN A JOB

The findings cited in the first five chapters indicate that Appalachians who migrated to Cincinnati, and their children, have not been included in the competition for housing, education, occupations, and income. Their average attainments are lower than those of either other white migrants or whites who have lived in Cincinnati for at least three generations, and are approximately the same as those of blacks. Analysis of the attainment process indicates that, except for those few who come from higher-status families and obtain a college education, Appalachians do not have the same access to the good life that others have.

In this chapter, attention is turned from the search for socioeconomic security to social and political integration. Appalachians have often been characterized by their isolation — by their failure to become involved in the communities to which they have migrated (e.g., Giffin, 1956). This chapter analyzes their participation in voluntary organizations, in primary groups beyond the nuclear family, and in the political process. These kinds of participation are known to be related to socioeconomic status and to time in an area (Fellin and Litwak, 1963; Litwak, 1960). The observed rates of participation are adjusted for differences in education and number of years in Cincinnati, to see if an Appalachian background has an independent effect on social and political involvement. (Adjustments were made using an MCA procedure that is an application of analysis of covariance [Nie et al., 1975].)

VOLUNTARY-GROUP PARTICIPATION

Participants in the Cincinnati survey were asked whether they held membership in any of ten different kinds of voluntary organizations, or any other

TABLE 6.1
Voluntary-Group Participation of White Appalachians, White
Migrants from Other Areas, White Natives of Cincinnati, and Blacks
(figures unadjusted and adjusted for differences in
education and years in Cincinnati)
(in percent)

Organizational Membership	White Appalachian Migrants	Other White Migrants	Blacks	White Natives
Labor union	22	14*	27	17
Fraternal lodge	12	22*	14	19
Veterans' organization	9	11	7	10
Civic organization	12	23*	10	18
Youth-serving organization	10	19*	21*	20*
Civil rights organization	0	3*	10*	3*
Sport or hobby group	15	23	12	31*
Political organization	5	13*	5	12*
Professional association	10	18*	10	18
Social club	15	33*	15	28*
Other	10	16	16	12
Average number of memberships				
Unadjusted (eta = 0.17)	1.2	2.0*	1.5	1.9*
Adjusted (beta = 0.06)	1.5	1.8	1.7	1.8
Percent with no memberships				
Unadjusted (eta = 0.18)	42	25*	38	24*
Adjusted (beta = 0.08)	37	28	33	28

*Significantly different from percentages or averages for white Appalachian migrants
($p < .05$).

kinds of voluntary organizations we did not mention. Table 6.1 reports the
percentages of white Appalachians, white migrants from other areas, blacks, and
white natives who held membership in each type of organization. Except for
membership in labor unions, fewer Appalachians than other white migrants or
white natives were members of any of the different kinds of organizations.
Membership in labor unions is of course related to the type of work a person
does. Other whites are more likely to be employed in management or in profes-
sions which are typically nonunionized. Appalachians are more frequently
employed in semiskilled factory jobs where union membership is a custom
of employment.

For most types of organizations, participation rates of Appalachians are
similar to the participation rates of blacks. Blacks more frequently belong to

civil rights groups and to organizations which serve youth, but in other types of organizations, blacks and Appalachians participate at approximately the same rate. The failure of Appalachians to participate in civil rights organizations should not go unnoticed. For a number of years, blacks have recognized the need to organize in order to obtain power which will enable them to obtain access to jobs, housing, and other things which have been denied to them. Although the majority of blacks do not join such groups, sufficient numbers do, such that they have become a factor in the decision-making process nationally and locally. Those who would explain the lack of such organizations among Appalachians by citing their reluctance to join groups should take note that blacks are no less reluctant but are much more organized.

Among Appalachians, the average number of organizational memberships is lowest and the percentage belonging to no organizations is highest. Appalachians belong to an average of 1.2 organizations, while white migrants from other areas belong to an average of 2.0 and white natives an average of 1.9, or approximately 50 percent more. The average memberships of blacks are approximately the same as those of Appalachians: 42 percent of Appalachians and 38 percent of blacks belong to no organizations, compared to 24 percent of the Cincinnati natives and 25 percent of the white migrants from other places.

Most of the difference in affiliation rates appears to be explained by differences in socioeconomic status and in years in Cincinnati. When membership rates are adjusted for these differences, the four groups are approximately the same, with white Appalachians averaging only slightly fewer memberships than people in other groups. About half the difference disappears when percentages having no memberships are adjusted. Adjusted percentages show 37 percent of Appalachians and 33 percent of blacks with no memberships, compared to 28 percent of other white migrants and white Cincinnati natives. Although Appalachians affiliate even less than other groups when differences in education and time in Cincinnati are taken into account, the differences are not especially substantial.

While Appalachians join voluntary organizations about as often as people in other groups, they do not appear to join the same groups that these other people do. Labor unions are the only type of voluntary organization to which a substantial proportion of Appalachians belonged: almost a fourth of the Appalachians interviewed were union members. White migrants from other areas and white Cincinnati natives were more likely to belong to social and recreational organizations: 33 percent of the white migrants from other areas and 28 percent of the Cincinnati natives listed memberships in social clubs; 23 percent and 31 percent, respectively, were members of sports or hobby groups; and 22 percent and 19 percent, respectively, belonged to fraternal lodges. In each case these percentages are approximately twice those of Appalachians or blacks. The other type of voluntary organization to which other white migrants and Cincinnati natives belonged was civic organizations: 23 percent and 18 percent, respectively, listed membership in civic organizations; 19 percent and 20 percent, respectively, were members of youth-serving organizations; and 13 percent and 12 percent, respectively, were members of political organizations. Again these membership rates are twice those of Appalachians, although blacks participate in such organizations about as often as other white migrants or Cincinnati natives, especially when civil rights organizations are included. In the types of groups Appalachians join, they show some similarity to blacks but little similarity to either other white migrants or white Cincinnati natives. They remain largely isolated from participation with non-Appalachian people.

A similar pattern of participation is observed among religious organizations. Appalachians belong to different religious organizations. When asked their denomination, only 8 percent of the Appalachians stated they were not a part of any religious group; this percentage is lower as compared to the percentage of other white migrants and about the same as that found among blacks or white Cincinnati natives. They appear to have found churches in the Cincinnati area with which they have affiliated.

The majority of Appalachians have joined fundamentalist Baptist and Holiness churches in the Cincinnati area: 31 percent were Baptist church members and 21 percent were Holiness. All other Protestant churches combined drew only 27 percent of the Appalachians, and most of these were either Methodist church members (10 percent) or Presbyterian (8 percent). Another 13 percent were Catholic. Roscoe Giffin (1956) theorized that urban churches, with their emphases on social gospel, were not attractive to Appalachians. He appears to have been right. Appalachians are clearly drawn to fundamentalist groups, which stress salvation and adherence to doctrine. For the most part, these denominations were the groups among which Appalachians were raised, either in Cincinnati for second-generation migrants or in Appalachia: 23 percent of the Appalachians reported their parents were Holiness and 39 percent said parents were Baptist. Only 3 percent of the Appalachians are presently Holiness or Baptist, after being raised among some other group. Appalachians have either found or established churches in Cincinnati that are similar to those in which they were raised.

Only 14 percent of the other white migrants and 10 percent of the Cincinnati natives were Holiness, and only 5 percent and 3 percent, respectively, were Baptist. Catholicism is the dominant religion of both of these groups. More than a third of the other white migrants (35 percent) and almost two-thirds of the Cincinnati natives (64 percent) were Catholic. The remainder were mostly members of nonfundamentalist Protestant churches. Even after adjusting for differences in education and years in Cincinnati, major differences exist between the types of church to which Appalachians and other white groups belong.

The types of churches which attract Appalachians are the same types which attract blacks. Indeed, 14 percent of the blacks were Holiness and 52 percent were Baptist. However, it is extremely doubtful that Appalachians and blacks worship together. These fundamentalist churches tend to be highly segregated along racial lines. They believe the same doctrine but each group establishes its own churches.

TABLE 6.2

Religious Participation of White Appalachians, White Migrants from Other Areas, White Natives of Cincinnati, and Blacks
(figures unadjusted and adjusted for differences in education and years in Cincinnati)
(in percent)

Participation	White Appalachian Migrants	Other White Migrants	Blacks	White Natives
Religious denomination				
Unadjusted				
Catholic	13	35*	10*	64*
Holiness	21	14	14	10
Baptist	31	5	52	3
Other Protestant	27	29	18	17
Jewish	0	4	0	0
None	8	13	7	6
Adjusted				
Holiness	21	13*	14	10
Baptist	28	6	51	6
Other	51	81	35	84
Frequency of attendance				
Unadjusted (eta = 0.12)	1.6	1.8	2.0*	2.0*
Adjusted (beta = 0.10)	1.7	1.8	2.1*	1.9
Nonworship participation				
Unadjusted (eta = 0.20)	11	25*	36*	19
Adjusted (beta = 0.20)	12	25*	36	18
Religious office				
Unadjusted (eta = 0.18)	5	11	20*	6
Adjusted (beta = 0.19)	6	10	22*	6

*Significantly different from percentages or averages for white Appalachian migrants (p < .05).

Although Appalachians affiliate with religious groups as often as do people in other groups, they do not participate as actively. Participants in the Cincinnati survey were asked whether they attended religious services more than once a week (such attendance was given a score of 4), once a week (3), a few times a month (2), a few times a year (1), or never (0). Appalachians had the lowest average attendance of any group — an average attendance score of 1.6 compared to 1.8 for other white migrants, 2.0 for blacks, and 2.0 for Cincinnati natives. Even after adjustments for differences in education and years in Cincinnati, most of the difference in frequency of attendance remained. Appalachians are also less likely to have any participation in religious organizations other than the attending of religious services. Only 11 percent cited such participation, compared to 36 percent of the blacks, 25 percent of the other white migrants, and 19 percent of the Cincinnati natives. Adjustments for differences in education and years in Cincinnati failed to change these differences. Finally, Appalachians were less likely than people in other groups to hold a position of leadership in their churches. Only 5 percent of the Appalachians stated they held either an office or other position of responsibility in any religious organization. This compared to 11 percent of other white migrants and 20 percent of the blacks. Few Cincinnati natives held religious offices, but they were members of a religious group which depends upon professional leaders instead of lay volunteers. Much more than other groups, Appalachians appear to maintain nominal participation in their churches as opposed to taking an active role.

At first blush, then, it appeared that overall, the pattern of participation in voluntary organizations demonstrated the integration of Appalachians into the mainstream of Cincinnati life. Once adjustments were made for differences in education and years in Cincinnati, Appalachians were as likely as others to hold memberships in voluntary organizations and to average as many memberships. Upon closer inspection, it becomes clear that Appalachians are participating in groups which non-Appalachians seldom join. Appalachians are most likely to join labor unions and fundamentalist Protestant churches. Other whites are more likely to join social groups, civic organizations, and Catholic and liberal Protestant churches. Not only do Appalachians join different groups, but they participate less actively in the groups they join. A comparison of religious participation demonstrated that Appalachians attended religious services less frequently, less often participated outside of religious services, and less often took positions of responsibility. They appear to be more isolated overall than their membership rates would indicate. Few hold more than nominal membership. Appalachians remain isolated not because they are reluctant to join voluntary associations, but because the organizations they join are different and their participation is limited.

SCHOOL PARTICIPATION

Participation at the child's school demonstrates an ability or willingness to interact with one of the large bureaucracies which characterize urban institutions.

Urban schools are large and relatively impersonal. They must cope with the needs of thousands of students and therefore must rely upon standardized procedures, bounded interactions, and formal communication. While these institutions are common in urban areas, they have been held to repel Appalachians who have moved from rural areas. Participants in the Cincinnati survey who had children in school were asked three questions about their involvement in the school — whether they belonged to the PTA, whether they had attended any meetings during the year, and whether they had had any contact with any of their children's teachers. These three items were summed to form an index of participation.

Table 6.3 presents the average participation score for each group and the percentage who had no participation at their children's schools. On either measure, Appalachians have less involvement than parents in the other groups. Their average school participation score was 1.3 compared to 1.8 for other white migrants and 1.5 for blacks and Cincinnati natives. Further, 26 percent of the Appalachians had no participation at their children's schools, which is considerably higher than the 14 percent of other white migrants and blacks and the 13 percent of white Cincinnati natives. Even after adjusting for differences in education and years in Cincinnati, Appalachians are much less involved in their children's schools than are parents of other children.

TABLE 6.3
School Participation of White Appalachians, White Migrants from Other Areas, White Natives of Cincinnati, and Blacks Who Have Children in School
(figures unadjusted and adjusted for differences in education and years in Cincinnati)

Participation	White Appalachian Migrants	Other White Migrants	Blacks	White Natives
Average school participation				
Unadjusted (eta = 0.20)	1.3	1.8*	1.5	1.5
Adjusted (beta = 0.18)	1.2	1.7*	1.6	1.7*
Percent with no participation				
Unadjusted (eta = 0.14)	26	14	14	13
Adjusted (beta = 0.20)	27	18	12	7*
Number of cases	67	80	49	47

*Significantly different from percentages or averages for white Appalachian migrants ($p < .05$).

Two interpretations seem possible. Either Appalachians do not recognize the importance of education or they have difficulty interacting with the types of institutions in which education takes place. The fact that they have a high dropout rate would seem to indicate that they do not recognize the importance of education. However, 67 percent of those who had failed to finish high school felt they needed more education than they had; 63 percent of those with children in school wanted their children to obtain more than a high school education, and only 2 percent said they would let their children quit if the child had a chance to get a good job. Appalachians at least verbalize the importance of education.

It seems more probable that parents of Appalachian children have difficulty interacting in the types of institutions where their children are educated. There is little in their background which would equip them with skills for such inter- action. Their jobs are relatively routine and require a minimum of interaction with others. They work with things and not with people. Their participation in voluntary organizations is largely limited to membership. Their churches are often small and more like primary groups than institutions. As a result, Appa- lachians have not had experiences which would give them skills to interact in bureaucratic settings. That lack of experience may result in fears which make involvement in their children's schools difficult.

POLITICAL PARTICIPATION

If a group is to have any influence, its members must be involved in the political process. Those of us who are old enough recall the summers dozens of young people spent in Alabama, Mississippi, and other southern states, convincing blacks to register to vote and fighting competency exams designed to prevent their registration. The effort paid off and today blacks exercise considerable political power both nationally and locally. Few politicians seeking election to office fail to consider the concerns of black people. Their votes are sufficient to alter the outcome of many elections. The same cannot be said for Appalachian migrants and their children.

Participants in the Cincinnati survey were asked if they voted in the 1974 elections. Those who did not were asked if they were registered to vote. The results are shown in Table 6.4. Fewer Appalachians than any other group had voted in the 1974 elections: Only 41 percent of the Appalachians, compared to 70 percent of other white migrants, 69 percent of white natives, and 62 percent of the blacks, had voted. Even after adjustments for differences in education and years in Cincinnati, Appalachians were considerably underrepresented at the polls. Almost half of the Appalachians were not even registered to vote. This percentage is more than twice the percentage of other white groups and consid- erably greater than that of blacks.

The failure of Appalachians to participate even minimally in the political process maintains their isolation from the mainstream of Cincinnati. Appalachians

TABLE 6.4

Political Participation of White Appalachians, White Migrants from Other Areas, White Natives of Cincinnati, and Blacks
(figures unadjusted and adjusted for differences in education and years in Cincinnati)
(in percent)

Participation in 1974 Elections	White Appalachian Migrants	Other White Migrants	Blacks	White Natives
Unadjusted				
Not registered	49	21*	30*	21*
Registered, not voting	9	10	8	10
Voting	41	70	62	69
Adjusted				
Not voting	50	32*	33*	39
Voting	50	68	67	61

*Significantly different from percentages for white Appalachian migrants (p < .05).

need many of the services politicians can provide. They need job-training programs both to reduce unemployment, especially among the children of migrants, and to upgrade the level of jobs obtained. Local CETA programs direct efforts to finding jobs for blacks; local governments set aside positions for blacks in both fire and police departments; construction contracts are held for blacks in skilled trades. This has had the desired effect of producing great upward mobility among blacks.

An unfortunate side effect of this effort has been to classify Appalachians simply as white and to group them with other white migrants and Cincinnati natives. No special effort is made to place an Appalachian CETA worker or to hire an Appalachian police officer or to provide Appalachians with remedial education programs. An Appalachian in these programs would show up in a report simply as a white and the conclusion would be drawn that the groups needing assistance were denied. Yet it has been demonstrated that Appalachians are more similar in needs to blacks in Cincinnati than they are to either other white migrants or Cincinnati natives.

Why should a local politician respond to the needs of Appalachians? Few Appalachians can afford sizable campaign contributions and few are in positions which yield influence. The major source of political influence in the short run is the number of political votes a politician can expect in return for the delivery of services. If half the Appalachians are not even registered to vote, then there is little a politician can expect to receive as an advocate for Appalachians.

Appalachians may fail to register to vote because they have difficulty dealing with the process or because they feel alienated. In 1975 a person had to register several weeks before an election. This required an action prior to the interest most elections would generate. To register, the person had to interact with another representative of an urban institution who, in a secondary fashion, asked questions and filled out forms. At least some evidence suggests such an experience would deter many Appalachians. Other Appalachians may not register because they feel voting is pointless. Such alienation among Appalachians is demonstrated in the following chapter.

PRIMARY-GROUP PARTICIPATION

Primary groups are often seen as an alternative to secondary associations, and the finding that people in a group fail to participate in secondary groups is taken as evidence of their strong primary ties. Such is typical of many descriptions of Appalachian migrants. They are said to avoid interaction in formal groups based upon secondary relationships and to develop strong primary ties especially among family members.

Some of the findings already presented in this book cast doubt about the presence of especially strong family ties among Appalachians. In Chapter 3 it was observed that Appalachians were not more likely than people in other groups to choose a place to live where they could be close to family. Blacks and Cincinnati natives were much more likely than Appalachians to choose housing because it was close to family. Proximity to work and quality of housing were more important to Appalachians than family was. Second, Appalachians were the least likely to have moved to Cincinnati because other family members were there. The opportunity to work was the almost universal explanation Appalachians gave for migrating to Cincinnati. Third, in Chapter 5 it was found that Appalachians were not more dependent on family ties to find work than were blacks and were less dependent than Cincinnati natives. They did go out of town more often to visit relatives but still averaged only four visits a year. These findings suggest that Appalachians do not develop strong primary-group ties with family members in lieu of more secondary-group participation.

Information about two other primary-group activities was obtained from participants in the Cincinnati survey and shed light on the involvement of Appalachians. First, Appalachians and others who had relatives living in the Cincinnati area were asked if they got together with any of these relatives a few times a year or less (for which the score given was 0), once every month or two (a score of 1), a few times a month (2), about once a week (3), or more than once a week (4). Table 6.5 demonstrates that there are no differences in the frequency with which an average person in the various groups gets together with relatives in the area. Appalachians, blacks, Cincinnati natives, and other white migrants all get together with relatives between a few times a month and once

TABLE 6.5

Primary-Group Participation of White Appalachians, White Migrants from Other Areas, White Natives of Cincinnati, and Blacks (figures unadjusted and adjusted for differences in education and years in Cincinnati)

Participation	White Appalachian Migrants	Other White Migrants	Blacks	White Natives
Visits with relatives in area				
Unadjusted (eta = 0.02)	2.2	2.3	2.3	2.2
Adjusted (beta = 0.06)	2.1	2.3	2.3	2.3
Number of cases	120	124	86	131
Participation in neighborhood				
Unadjusted (eta = 0.12)	0.36	0.43	0.54*	0.46
Adjusted (beta = 0.13)	0.40	0.41	0.58*	0.42

*Significantly different from averages for white Appalachian migrants ($p < .05$).

a week. There is no evidence anywhere in this study that Appalachians develop especially strong extended family ties or stronger ties than people in other groups develop.

Information was also obtained about participation in local neighborhoods. Participants were asked if, whenever people in their neighborhoods got together to get things done, they never took an active part (given a score of 0), took part only part of the time (1), or all of the time (2). Table 6.5 indicates that Appalachians have the lowest neighborhood participation score of any group and blacks the highest. After adjusting for differences in education and years in Cincinnati, Appalachians appear to be as involved in their neighborhoods as are other whites, but considerably less involved than blacks.

Overall, there is only slight reason to believe that Appalachians have weaker primary-group ties than people in other groups, but there is no evidence that primary groups are stronger among Appalachians.

SUMMARY

This survey of the participation of Appalachians in primary and secondary groups further demonstrates the isolation of Appalachians from other groups in Cincinnati. First, their level of participation in secondary groups is lower than the participation of any other group. They are most likely to have no memberships in voluntary groups, to have fewer average memberships, and to participate only nominally if they do hold memberships. They are the least likely to vote in an election and the most likely to be unregistered. They have the lowest involvement in their children's school system. Except for memberships in voluntary groups, the absence of participation among Appalachians remains even after adjustments for differences in education and years in Cincinnati. Clearly, Appalachians are isolated by their lack of secondary-group participation, and that isolation cannot be attributed to lower socioeconomic status or recency in the area.

Second, Appalachians who do participate in secondary groups are more likely to participate in groups with other Appalachians than in groups which other people join. Appalachians are most likely to participate in labor unions or in Holiness and Baptist denominations. Other whites are unlikely to be members of these groups, instead preferring membership in social groups, civic groups, and Catholic churches. Blacks also hold memberships in labor unions and in Baptist and Holiness denominations but are probably segregated from Appalachians and other whites. Preferences for different groups also remain unaffected when controlling for education and years in Cincinnati.

Third, the isolation of Appalachians portrayed in secondary associations is not offset by primary relationships. Appalachians are not more likely than other groups to maintain extended family ties in the area and on some measures appear to have weaker ties. Other groups are more involved in neighborhood affairs than are Appalachians. Whether studied from the perspective of secondary associations or of primary groups, Appalachians appear to be the most isolated group in the area.

7

HEADACHES AND HEARTBREAKS

The difficulty Appalachians have experienced in the competition for economic well-being, and their failure to participate fully in the community where they have moved, may well have created further problems. This chapter focuses attention upon how Appalachians feel about their lives, what problems have emerged, and the present state of their psychological well-being. Because many of these variables are related to socioeconomic position, differences between Appalachians and other groups will be adjusted for differences in educational attainment.

FEELINGS OF RELATIVE DEPRIVATION

People evaluate where they stand in society and they interpret that position as just or unjust. Impressions of justice are based on people's perceptions of what they have contributed and their perceptions of what other people receive for their contributions. For example, if a college education is believed to be a prerequisite to obtaining a job in management, then a person who chooses not to go to college is unlikely to develop negative feelings when someone else is made manager. On the other hand, if a person is denied the opportunity to go to college for a nonacademic reason, that person may resent not being a manager. Similarly, if two people do the same task equally well, one worker is unlikely to be satisfied with having a lower wage than another, irrespective of any rationale that may be offered. Norms of "reciprocity" (Gouldner, 1960) or "distributive justice" (Runciman, 1966) emerge in each social system that specify the standard, or fair, reward an individual has a right to expect. When that reward is not forthcoming, feelings of relative deprivation emerge (Runciman, 1966).

100

Participants in the Cincinnati survey were asked to evaluate whether they were worse off than, about the same as, or better off than most Americans in terms of housing, income, job security, and general standing in the community. Scores of 0, 1, and 2 were assigned to responses, respectively, and the numbers summed to form a scale ranging from 0 to 8 with a reliability of 0.84. Table 7.1 indicates that, based upon this scale, Appalachians perceive themselves as doing not nearly as well as other white migrants or white Cincinnati natives perceive themselves as doing and only slightly better than blacks believe they are doing. Adjustments for differences in education diminish this difference only slightly.

People's perceptions of their standing in a community are affected by their choice of reference group. Previous studies have demonstrated that Appalachians who migrated to midwestern cities have done better than they were doing in Appalachia and are doing better than Appalachians who did not migrate (Morgan, 1981; Photiadis, 1981). This suggests that Appalachian migrants would have a positive evaluation of their standing in the community since they have experienced considerable upward mobility and are doing better than nonmigrants with whom they were raised. However, Appalachians' perceptions of their standing in society parallel their relative attainments in their area of destination. In Chapter 3 it was seen that Appalachians have much lower attainments than either other white migrants or Cincinnati natives and only slightly higher attainments

TABLE 7.1
Relative Deprivation among White Appalachians, White Migrants from Other Areas, White Natives of Cincinnati, and Blacks
(figures unadjusted and adjusted for differences in education)

Deprivation Measure	White Appalachian Migrants	Other White Migrants	Blacks	White Natives
Perceived standing in community				
Unadjusted (eta = 0.27)	4.6	5.5*	4.2	5.3*
Adjusted (beta = 0.19)	4.8	5.4*	4.4	5.2
Perceived opportunity				
Unadjusted (eta = 0.36)	6.0	6.5	3.9*	6.3
Adjusted (beta = 0.29)	6.3	6.3	4.2*	6.1
Satisfaction with standing				
Unadjusted (eta = 0.23)	4.5	5.4*	4.0	5.1*
Adjusted (beta = 0.21)	4.6	5.4*	4.0	5.0

*Significantly different from averages for white Appalachian migrants ($p < .05$).

than blacks. Their perceived relative standing is identical to their actual relative attainment in Cincinnati. This suggests that Appalachians who migrated moved roots and all: The evaluation of success is not based on how friends who stayed behind are doing or on what people would expect if they had not migrated. Relative success is based upon a comparison with others who live in the place where Appalachians migrated.

Participants in the survey were asked their perceptions of their opportunity to get ahead. They were asked how often they had a fair chance to get the kind of job, earn the amount of income, and obtain the education they desired; responses and scores assigned were: hardly ever (0), only part of the time (1), most of the time (2), or all of the time (3). Responses were summed to form a scale ranging from 0 to 9 with a reliability of 0.84. The responses of Appalachians were almost identical to those of other whites, especially when differences in education were taken into account. On the average, whites in the study, including Appalachians, felt they had had an opportunity most of the time. Blacks, on the other hand, believed that they had been given much less of an opportunity than whites believed they had been given. Even after differences in education were taken into account, typically blacks believed they had been given a chance to get ahead only part of the time.

The difference in the perception of opportunity among Appalachians and among blacks is interesting. Both groups have almost identical attainments and almost identical perceptions of their attainments. However, Appalachians are much more likely to believe that they have had an opportunity in society. This difference may be symptomatic of a difference in the tendency to place blame. Blacks may see that racist practices in society deny them a fair chance to get ahead much of the time. Appalachians may have a greater tendency to blame themselves. This difference may account for some of the differences observed earlier. Because blacks see society as responsible for what has happened, they have engaged in political action to bring about social change. They are more likely to join political action groups and to participate in the electoral process. Appalachians have a greater trust in society and therefore perceive less of a need to take political action to redress grievances. In the short run, Appalachians create fewer problems for society because they do not pressure it to change, but in the long run, needed changes are unlikely to occur without pressure.

People not only evaluate what they have obtained in society, but how satisfied they are with those attainments. Participants in the Cincinnati survey were asked how satisfied they were with their job, their housing, their income, and their job security. Responses were scored 0, 1, or 2, with 2 indicating the most satisfied, and a summated scale was created with a reliability of 0.89. Table 7.1 indicates that Appalachians were much less satisfied than other white groups and only slightly more satisfied than blacks even after differences in education were taken into account.

Taken together, these findings are indicative of an emerging social problem among Appalachians. They clearly do not perceive themselves as doing very well compared to other people, and the findings confirm that they are not doing very well. While they believe that they have had an opportunity to get ahead in life, they remain dissatisfied with what they have obtained. It is unlikely that they will riot in the street or even take milder action which would draw attention to their plight, since they don't seem to feel that anyone else is to blame. However, they moved to Cincinnati to get ahead, they don't feel they have gotten ahead, and they feel dissatisfied with their present achievements. That conflict creates the basis for the emergence of some serious problems.

LEGAL PROBLEMS

While the majority of Appalachians in Cincinnati do not dwell in inner-city slums (and never have), they are disproportionately poor and are dispropor-tionately found in lower-income neighborhoods. Some have argued that the frustration such a life style brings and the exposure to deviant role models have caused many Appalachians to participate in acts which bring them into contact with the police and courts (Huelsman, 1969). Others argue that because they live in low-income neighborhoods and because police harbor negative stereo-types about them, they face a higher probability of arrest for minor offenses or for offenses they did not commit (Maloney and Huelsman, 1972; Reeves, 1976).

Participants in the survey were asked whether they had ever been arrested for something other than a traffic violation. Thirteen percent of the Appalachians reported a record of arrests. This percentage is about twice the percentage of

TABLE 7.2
Legal Problems among White Appalachians, White Migrants from Other Areas, White Natives of Cincinnati, and Blacks
(figures unadjusted and adjusted for differences in education)

Problem	White Appalachian Migrants	Other White Migrants	Blacks	White Natives
Percent arrested				
Unadjusted (eta = 0.17)	13	5	19	7
Adjusted (beta = 0.16)	13	6	19	7
Support for law				
Unadjusted (eta = 0.21)	13.5	13.1	11.0*	12.9
Adjusted (beta = 0.22)	13.4	13.2	10.9*	13.0

*Significantly different from average for white Appalachian migrants (p < .05).

other whites who have been arrested and about 6 percent less than the percentage of blacks. Interestingly, adjusting for differences in education as a measure of socioeconomic status failed to change the relative arrest records among groups.

It is impossible to determine why Appalachians have a higher arrest record than other groups, except to note that it is not because they are more likely to be of lower socioeconomic status. Appalachians may more frequently engage in acts of violence and other crimes which cause them to be arrested. Many of them have reason to feel angry. We have seen that, except for those few who come from middle-class origins and possess a good education, they do not compete effectively for jobs and pay in the Cincinnati area. They see other whites with similar backgrounds and identical educations getting better jobs and earning higher wages. In this same vein, blacks, who have the highest rate of arrest, are the least likely to be hired.

It is just as possible that Appalachians are the recipients of negative stereotypes among police. McCoy and Watkins (1981) have demonstrated that jokes told in Cincinnati reveal widespread negative stereotypes among the general population, including stereotypes about their attraction to certain kinds of crime. Maloney and Huelsman (1972) cite a Cincinnati police report which indicates that those negative impressions about Appalachians are found among the police as well. A police officer has to use a lot of judgment. An argument can be broken up and participants told to go separate ways; a drunk can be sent home in a taxi; parents can be called for a youth found shoplifting. The decision made is affected by the impression held about the people the officer is dealing with. If police officers believe negative stereotypes about Appalachians, then they may more often resort to arrest.

Although Appalachians have higher rates of arrests than other groups, except blacks, they are more supportive of the legal system than are members of any other group. A series of seven questions was used to measure attitudes toward the legal system. Those ranged from the belief that police stop and search people without reason, to the belief that it is right to break the law to support your family. The summated scale had a reliability of .70. Appalachians had the highest average score, demonstrating greatest group support for the law, although once differences in education were taken into account, their support was identical to the support of other white groups. Blacks, on the other hand, demonstrated more negative attitudes toward the police and courts.

This pattern, while appearing contradictory, is consistent with the previous data on relative deprivation. Appalachians have lower attainments and yet feel they have had adequate opportunity; they have more frequent arrests and yet continue to believe the legal system is just. They clearly appear to internalize blame for what happens to them. They don't seem to react to an arrest with feelings that the police officer didn't have to do it. Whatever they were doing that caused them to be arrested appears to be taken as sufficient justification for their arrest and subsequent treatment by the courts. Blacks, who are more likely to blame the system for their lack of economic achievement, are also more likely to feel the legal system is unfair.

FAMILY PROBLEMS

Within the families of the Appalachians, evidence begins to emerge that the stresses we have observed have taken their toll. Participants in the survey were asked how often they had a fight with their spouses, refused to speak to their spouses, swore at their spouses, and told their spouses they did not love them. Responses of never (given a score of 0), once a year or less (1), a few times a year (2), a few times a month (3), and once a week or more (4) were summed to form a scale with a reliability of .82. Table 7.3 shows that the average score of Appalachians was one full point above the average for other white groups. Adjustments for education failed to reduce this difference. Only blacks demonstrated greater stress in their marriages than was demonstrated among Appalachians.

The validity of the stress scale is indicated by the relative frequency of divorce within the different groups. Participants in the survey were asked their current marital status and those who were married were asked whether they had been married before. Persons who were divorced or separated at the time of the survey, or who were married before were scored as having had a disrupted marriage. Cincinnati natives had the fewest instances of disrupted marriages and blacks most of them. While Appalachians had only about half as many disrupted marriages as blacks, their rate of divorces and separations was greater than the rate of either of the other white groups and more than twice the rate of Cincinnati natives. Whether based on the relationship with their current spouses or on separation from a previous spouse, data show Appalachians clearly have more marital problems than other white groups.

Economic difficulties frequently result in conflicts between husbands and wives (Scanzoni, 1972). If a family doesn't have enough money, spouses frequently disagree over how the available money should be spent. Spouses may blame each other because the money isn't enough. If the wage earner feels it is somehow his or her fault because they don't have enough money, the problem is only complicated. Such feelings serve to make the person defensive and unable to maintain a healthy relationship with a spouse. If, in addition, the wage earner's identity is tied to the ability to provide, then self-respect is lost when earnings are too low, and either the family must accept the life style a low income provides or both spouses must bring in money.

This combination of factors may well be what has happened among Appalachians in Cincinnati. First, their average family income is well below the average income of other white groups. Many of them have had to resort to welfare in order to make ends meet. Second, we have just looked at findings which suggest that Appalachians tend to blame themselves for their problems. This feeling of guilt may well result in expressions of hostility. Finally, we have seen evidence that in the typical Appalachian family, the husband is the sole wage earner. If the wife also works and the family, as a result, has a higher income, stresses may still result if either spouse feels or both feel the husband alone should be able to earn enough for the family.

TABLE 7.3
Family Stress among White Appalachians, White Migrants from Other Areas, White Natives of Cincinnati, and Blacks
(figures unadjusted and adjusted for differences in education)

Stress Measure	White Appalachian Migrants	Other White Migrants	Blacks	White Natives
Stress with spouse				
Unadjusted (eta = 0.21)	4.0	3.0*	4.8	3.0*
Adjusted (beta = 0.21)	4.0	3.0	4.8	3.0
Number of cases	105	140	61	94
Stress with child				
Unadjusted (eta = 0.10)	3.6	2.7*	2.9	3.0
Adjusted (beta = 0.12)	3.7	2.7*	3.0	3.0
Number of cases	113	151	77	86
Percent with marital disruptions				
Unadjusted (eta = 0.31)	27	19	51*	11*
Adjusted (beta = 0.27)	25	22	48*	12*
Number of cases	130	171	84	104

*Significantly different from percentage or average for white Appalachian migrants ($p < .05$).

Stresses not only occur between husbands and wives. They also occur between parents and children. Parents in the survey were asked how often they fought with, swore at, or hit any of their children. Responses were summed to form a scale with a reliability of .81. The findings presented in Table 7.3 indicate that the stresses between Appalachians and their children are the greatest of any group, even when socioeconomic differences are taken into account.

The greater conflict between Appalachian parents and their children may occur because of a variety of reasons. It may be partly due to economic stresses which parents are experiencing. Just as they fight with spouses because they don't feel good about themselves, they may also fight with their children. It may also be more difficult to control children in cities than in smaller communities typical of Appalachia. Parents in cities often don't know the parents of their children's friends. Urban schools are more heterogeneous and expose the children to role models unfamiliar to parents. Children don't always understand why Appalachian parents may expect them to say "sir" and "ma'am", especially when their friends don't. Parents use their own childhood as a basis for how they want to raise their children. But that model may be unworkable or inappropriate for a person who has migrated from a rural area to a major city. For these reasons and others, Appalachians appear to experience greater stress in raising their children than do other parents.

We have been led to expect that we would find a strong family system among Appalachians, but we have not. The greater stress among Appalachian families suggests that once-strong families are perhaps disintegrating, or at least weakening. When the first migrants came to Cincinnati, they perhaps came from strong, supportive families. Over time, the stresses of trying to earn a living in an environment where they were not always welcome and were inadequately prepared took its toll. As a result, Appalachians living in Cincinnati in the 1970s frequently had to deal with dissolving marriages and, more often than most, had difficulty getting along with spouses and children.

PSYCHOLOGICAL PROBLEMS

Some people under stress express that tension by striking out. They blame other people for their troubles. The world, in some way, is seen as against them. Other people internalize that stress. Ulcers, allergies, and heart attacks result. They lose confidence in their ability to cope with life.

One indication of the internalization of stress is the occurrence of psycho-somatic illnesses. Participants in the survey were asked the frequency with which they experienced ten different ailments, including upset stomach, dizziness, perspiring hands, shortness of breath, nervousness, heart throbbing, sleepiness, and difficulty waking, working, and getting along with people because they did not feel well. Every person may have experienced most of these ailments some-time in the past, and some people may frequently experience one or two due to physical problems, but if a person experiences several such ailments on a regular basis, that is a good indication the person is suffering from stress. The number of different ailments a person experienced once in a while or fairly often was recorded as the measure of psychosomatic illness.

Table 7.4 indicates that Appalachians suffered from psychosomatic illness more frequently than members of any other group. They averaged 3.4 such ailments, which is an average of one ailment more than for other white migrants (2.6) or Cincinnati natives (2.4) and slightly more than for blacks (3.2). Adjusting for differences in socioeconomic status slightly reduced the differ-ence, but Appalachians continued to record more ailments than members of other groups. This supports the contention that Appalachians are more likely to internalize tension as opposed to directing it toward others. They are dissatisfied with what they have obtained in life and blame themselves for their failures. This becomes expressed in more psychosomatic illnesses than are found among other groups of people.

Appalachians also demonstrate higher levels of anomie than other white groups. Anomie reflects a feeling that the individual is unable to exercise control

TABLE 7.4
Psychological Stress among White Appalachians, White Migrants from Other Areas, White Natives of Cincinnati, and Blacks
(figures unadjusted and adjusted for differences in education)

Stress Measure	White Appalachian Migrants	Other White Migrants	Blacks	White Natives
Psychosomatic illnesses				
Unadjusted (eta = 0.17)	3.4	2.6*	3.2	2.4*
Adjusted (beta = 0.12)	3.2	2.8	3.0	2.5*
Anomie				
Unadjusted (eta = 0.37)	8.1	5.9*	9.9*	6.2*
Adjusted (beta = 0.27)	7.6	6.3*	9.3*	6.5*
Alcohol abuse				
Unadjusted (eta = 0.09)	8	6	5	12
Adjusted (beta = 0.09)	8	6	6	12
Number of cases	83	150	73	117

*Significantly different from average for white Appalachian migrants ($p < .05$).

over events. The world is seen as a hostile place and getting worse, making the future uncertain, if not threatening. In this study, anomie was measured using Srole's (1956) scale with a reliability of .86. On a scale of 0 to 15, with 15 indicating higher levels of anomie, Appalachians had an average score of 8.1. This is substantially higher than the 5.9 average for other white migrants or the 6.2 average for Cincinnati natives, but lower than the 9.9 average for blacks. Adjusting for educational differences reduced differences between groups only slightly.

Irrespective of the cause, anomie can result if an individual feels unable to control events. People who believe others are to blame and people who blame themselves may both develop anomie. Its importance lies in the prognosis for the future. Once a person becomes anomic, it is difficult to continue to try to do better. If people believe they can't get off welfare, can't get a better job, can't move to a better house, or can't get through school, then those people become resigned to where they are. Irrespective of the amount of opportunity or the competence of the individual, unless people believe they are able to succeed, few will try to do better.

It is impossible to tell in a cross-sectional study, but it is reasonable that anomie has developed among Appalachians since migration. Appalachians came to Cincinnati in search of work. Most probably saw it as a place where they had an opportunity. They believed they could do better. Many failed to realize their dreams and a higher-than-average level of dissatisfaction has resulted. If these people had originally had the high level of anomie demonstrated, it is doubtful they would have been motivated to migrate. That anomie developed because their aspirations were unfilled.

As a result of higher levels of anomie, the lower attainments among Appalachians may be self-perpetuating. Fewer Appalachians will be motivated to try to do better, believing the attempt would fail. Even more important, they may find it difficult to encourage their children. While they may wish their children could obtain a college education or a better job, they may feel that is really impossible. They feel powerless to intervene while their children leave school (these number 41 percent of second-generation Appalachians), become unemployed (11 percent of second-generation Appalachians) or employed in a lower-status job (58 percent of second-generation Appalachians), and go on welfare (28 percent of second-generation Appalachians). A cycle of poverty is established.

A final demonstration of psychological stress is found in the frequency of alcohol abuse. Participants in the Cincinnati survey were asked if they drank, and, if so, if they got high, got drunk, or missed work in an average year because of drinking. Forty percent of the Appalachians were teetotalers, which was considerably higher than the rate of nondrinkers in other groups. This is probably related to their membership in fundamentalist religious groups, which view alcohol consumption as a sin. Among those who did drink, Appalachians were not more likely than other groups to suffer from alcohol abuse, defined as missing work because of drinking. Only 8 percent of the Appalachians who drank missed work in an average year, compared to 6 percent of the other white migrants, 5 percent of blacks, and 12 percent of Cincinnati natives. The greater alcohol consumption among Cincinnati natives may result from the city's former role as the leading beer producer in the United States, or because Cincinnati was settled by people from European countries where alcohol consumption is higher than average. In any case, Appalachians do not suffer from alcohol abuse more frequently than other groups.

SUMMARY

The move to Cincinnati has been a dissatisfying experience for many Appalachians. They came in search of work, but lacked the education and class background which would give them access to middle-class jobs. They may have suffered discrimination because they were Appalachians. Asked to view their place in society, they recognized that they were worse off than other white groups in terms of income, education, job security, and standing in the community and expressed dissatisfaction over their lack of success. Only blacks had a lower perception of their attainments and showed greater dissatisfaction.

At the same time, Appalachians appear to blame themselves more than others for their failure to succeed. They are as likely as other whites to believe they had an opportunity to make it and are the most supportive of the legal system. Blacks, on the other hand, more frequently believe they have been denied an opportunity to get ahead and believe the legal system is unfair. On a day-to-day basis, the frustration among Appalachians probably creates few problems for local officials. They are unlikely to try to change the system, which they appear to trust.

The problems of Appalachians become expressed in family difficulties and personal stress. Despite earlier projections of strong Appalachian families, this study has consistently failed to find such evidence. It is more than possible that previously strong families have become weak as spouses take out their frustration on each other and the children. Appalachians in this study had higher-than-average marital disruptions and demonstrated greater conflict among spouses and children. It is the old story of the boss shouting at the employee, who goes home and shouts at the spouse, who shouts at the child, who kicks the dog. Stress also results in higher rates of psychosomatic illnesses and anomie as Appalachians develop physical symptoms of stress and accept life as something they cannot change.

8

ON THE WAY TO BECOMING
AN ETHNIC GROUP

Political activists and academic researchers continue to debate whether Appalachians should be classified as an ethnic group in the cities where they have migrated. Phillip Obermiller (1977) reviewed the extent of the controversy, making it clear that there is really no consensus. Some, such as James Branscome (1972) and Cratis Williams (1972), clearly believe that Appalachians are a culturally distinct group separate from the mainstream of America and from other cultural groups. Others. such as David Walls (1976), believe that the characteristics of Appalachians are class based rather than ethnic based. The majority stand somewhere in between — uncertain how best to characterize Appalachians in cities.

Part of the confusion is caused by the ambiguous definition of what constitutes an ethnic group. Wasvelod Isajiw (1974) surveyed 65 studies of ethnicity and found 27 different formal definitions. Additional confusion is caused by different characterizations of Appalachians. Bruce Ergood (1976) surveyed 20 studies of Appalachians and found only two agreeing on what were the important characteristics of Appalachians. Not a single characteristic was used in all of the studies. Given the lack of agreement over what an ethnic group is and the same lack of agreement over what is characteristic of Appalachians, it is no wonder that people come to different conclusions in evaluating the authenticity of characterizing Appalachians as an ethnic group.

The classification of Appalachians as an ethnic group is not without its political consequences. If Appalachian migrants were classified as an ethnic group, it would increase their power to compete as a group for goods and services which cities distribute. Not classifying Appalachians as an ethnic group means that every time an employer hires an Appalachian; every time the city adds an Appalachian to its police force; every time a social service agency assists an Appalachian; and every time an Appalachian is moved to a better school, the employer, city, agency, or school must report that it has placed a member of the dominant group, and recognized ethnic groups can use that information as evidence of discrimination against minorities. At the same time, to be recognized as an ethnic group means to accept oneself as different, and to seek goods and services on the basis of membership in an ethnic group means to accept that one is unable to compete without special assistance.

Opposition to the classification of Appalachians as an ethnic group can be expected from those who control the providing of goods and services and from those who are presently recognized as an ethnic group. Those who control delivery of goods and services have been forced over the past 25 years to increasingly justify their treatment of various groups — blacks, women, native Americans, Hispanics, the handicapped. As more and more groups seek recognition, those who control those decisions begin to make light of each new group, with responses such as, "Perhaps we should also give special consideration to . . ." Those who already receive special treatment because they are recognized as an ethnic group fear that the recognition of new groups will mean less for them. More than one meeting of different ethnic groups has broken down into a debate over whose needs are greatest, and no recognized ethnic group receiving special assistance has yet argued that it should share what it has received with an unrecognized ethnic group.

It is beyond the scope of any person to end this conflict and confusion. A more moderate objective is to review some of the criteria for recognition as an ethnic group and evaluate the characteristics of Appalachians against those criteria.

COMMON ORIGIN

According to Isajiw (1974), the most frequently cited attribute of ethnicity is a common national or geographic origin or common ancestry. That is probably more a matter of definition and does not in and of itself indicate the presence of an ethnic group. It is a necessary, but not a sufficient criterion. In this study, Appalachians have been defined as persons who were born, or had at least one parent who was born, in one of the 397 counties identified as the Appalachian region by the Appalachian Regional Commission.

The origins of Appalachians living in any area are much more concentrated. McCoy and Brown's (1981) analysis of migration streams in the 1940s, 1950s, and 1960s demonstrates that Appalachians living in different parts of the region migrated to different cities. Appalachians in Cincinnati migrated almost entirely from a seven-county area of southwestern Kentucky: 56 percent of the first-generation migrants who participated in this survey were born in Kentucky, and 66 percent of the Appalachian-born fathers and 58 percent of the Appalachian-born mothers of second-generation Appalachians migrated from the Appalachian portion of Kentucky.

Appalachia, ranging from New York in the north to Mississippi in the south, is home for a wide variety of people who probably have no more in common with each other than with people from outside the region. However, these findings demonstrate that migrants who find themselves living in the same city are likely to find other Appalachians from the same counties of Appalachia where they have their roots. This provides them a basis for group development that would not exist among Appalachians as a whole. They can share memories of childhood and relate news of such localized interest that it would only interest people who knew the places and the people involved. Ultimately, Appalachians migrating to a particular city may identify with one another as sharing a commonness unique to them.

It is important to realize that if Appalachians living in a midwestern city demonstrate characteristics of an ethnic group, people should not conclude that Appalachians in another city are a part of the same group. For example, Appalachians living in Cleveland moved from West Virginia. If Appalachians living in Cincinnati moved to Cleveland, they might feel no identity with Cleveland's Appalachians. We are not asking whether Appalachians, as a whole, should be recognized as an ethnic group. Instead, we are asking to what extent the Appalachians living in a single city do demonstrate characteristics of ethnic groups.

UNIQUE-CULTURE

The cultural-conflict theorists have popularized the idea that several groups within America have unique cultures which are separate from, and conflicting with, the dominant culture of the white middle class. Bruce Ergood (1976) reviewed 20 studies of Appalachians and found at least 11 different characteristics which were said to be traits of Appalachians. The most frequently cited were independence (12 studies), religious fundamentalism (8), strong family ties (7), living in harmony with nature (6), traditionalism (5), and fatalism (5). With the exception of living in harmony with nature, each of those traits was measured in the Cincinnati study. Two conclusions emerge.

First, traits which are said to be characteristic of Appalachians were neither unique to Appalachians nor particularly characteristic of them. Independence, indicated by the reluctance to submit oneself to the authority of others, and fatalism were weaker traits among Appalachians than among blacks, white Cincinnati natives, or white migrants from other places. The average scores of Appalachians were at the end of the scales, indicating relatively low levels of independence and fatalism. Appalachians were more traditionalistic than either Cincinnati natives or white migrants from other places, but were not more traditionalistic than were blacks.

The choice of churches suggests that Appalachians are indeed fundamentalists. Baptist and Holiness groups accounted for the choices of 52 percent of the Appalachians. Cincinnati natives and other white migrants were most frequently Catholic and almost never in Baptist or Holiness groups. While blacks were often Baptists, it seems certain that their churches are different from those of Appalachians.

Perhaps the biggest surprise in this study has been the inability to find evidence of strong family ties among the migrants. We were led to believe that Appalachians were drawn to Cincinnati by other relatives, but only 12 percent of the Appalachian participants (the lowest of any group) said they chose to move to Cincinnati because of family and 17 percent (lower than either blacks or Cincinnati natives) said they lived in their present neighborhood because it was close to family. While stories abound about migrants obtaining jobs through contacts provided by relatives, only 30 percent of the Appalachians in the labor force (again less than either blacks or Cincinnati natives) were assisted by their families. Even the stories of Appalachians going back home every weekend were offset by participants in this study, who averaged four visits a year to see relatives. Among nuclear families, 27 percent of the Appalachians who had ever married had been divorced at one time or another. Measures of stress in present families indicated that the Appalachians had the second highest frequency of stress with spouses and the highest with children. There was no indication at all in this study that Appalachians maintain strong relations with either extended- or nuclear-family members.

Not only was there little evidence of unique cultural traits among Appalachians, with the exception of religious fundamentalism; there was little to indicate that cultural traits said to be characteristic of Appalachians caused any conflict for migrants living in Cincinnati. Independence, fatalism, traditionalism, and dependency upon relatives, along with confidence in institutions, were included in the study of the educational and occupational attainment processes. The only variable substantially related to achievement was the effect of traditionalism upon educational attainment. Those Appalachians who subscribed to the value of traditionalism had less education than those who did not. It is just as reasonable, though, to conclude that traditionalism is the result, rather than the cause, of educational attainment. Traditionalism had no effect upon occupational attainment and neither did the other cultural values. Dependency upon relatives slightly reduced occupational attainment, but that dependency was the exception among Appalachians.

SOCIOECONOMIC HOMOGENEITY

Class differences are probably stronger than ethnic differences, and for a person to identify with another, it is necessary that their socioeconomic differences not be too great. Appalachians in Cincinnati possess highly similar socioeconomic levels in the areas of occupational, educational, and income attainment.

Some 69 percent of the Appalachians in the labor force were blue-collar workers and almost all of these were working in semiskilled or unskilled jobs. The majority of Cincinnati natives (61 percent) and white migrants from other places (66 percent) were white-collar workers, and those who were blue-collar workers were most often employed in skilled trades.

Further, 82 percent of the Appalachians surveyed have no education beyond high school and 46 percent left high school before graduation. Few whites in other groups failed to complete high school and almost half have additional years of education.

There is almost a $4,000 gap in the median incomes of Appalachians and other white groups. Almost half of the Appalachians had incomes below $11,000, while half of the other whites had incomes above $15,000. Put a different way, the average income of an Appalachian family living in Cincinnati is only 75 percent of the income of other whites. Some 53 percent of the Appalachians surveyed had received welfare benefits at some time or another and 20 percent were receiving benefits at the time of the survey.

The vast majority of Appalachians may best be described as lower working class. They are involved in jobs requiring few skills, have an inadequate number of years of education, and earn less-than-average incomes. These are just the opposite of what was found among other white groups. The differences are more than just a few percentage points. They are differences in the modal character- istics of the groups. Interaction between Appalachians most likely involves an exchange between equals, but interaction between Appalachians and non-Appa- lachians probably places the Appalachian in a subordinate position. To this extent, David Walls (1976) is correct when he says that Appalachian problems are problems of class.

Intergenerational Inheritance

Evidence that the experiences of Appalachians in Cincinnati are inade- quately addressed through a class analogy begins to be seen in the comparison of first- and second-generation migrants. Historically in the United States, as new white groups moved into an area, they came with a lower-than-average education and took the lowest-status and poorest-paying jobs. However, their children were able to obtain the necessary education and subsequently hold higher-status, better-paying jobs. By the time the third generation of migrants entered the labor force, they competed at parity with others. Only nonwhite groups failed to achieve an equal standing with other groups (Blau and Dun- can, 1967).

A comparison of first- and second-generation migrants suggests that the experiences of Appalachians are more similar to those of blacks than to those of other white groups. The second-generation Appalachians have done only a little better than the first generation in acquiring the necessary years of educa- tion to compete for good jobs. Some 41 percent of the second generation left school before high school graduation and only 21 percent went byond high school. They remain more than two years behind the average educational attain- ments of other white migrants or Cincinnati natives. The second-generation

Appalachians have done even worse than the first generation in the competition for jobs: 55 percent of the first-generation Appalachians and 58 percent of the second generation were employed in semiskilled or unskilled jobs. At the time of the survey, 3 percent of the first generation and 11 percent of the second were unemployed and looking for work. The median income of second-generation migrants is the same as the median income of the first ($11,250), although a lower percentage of second-generation Appalachians had incomes below $6,000; but second-generation migrants are more likely than first-generation Appalachians to be living in the inner city and to live in slightly worse neighborhoods.

Together, these figures indicate that Appalachians are not moving up the socioeconomic ladder. The second generation has not moved beyond the attainments of the first. Instead of assimilating into the economic life of Cincinnati, they appear to be trapped in a self-perpetuating cycle, going nowhere. The absence of that assimilation suggests that Appalachians are a group apart from the mainstream of Cincinnati.

SEPARATE PROCESSES OF ACHIEVEMENT

It has long been recognized that members of minority racial and ethnic groups are not rewarded in the same way that members of the dominant group are. For that reason, the 1964 Civil Rights Act forbade discrimination against ethnic minorities in the competition for education, occupation, and income. However, ethnic groups cited were restricted to blacks, native Americans, and the foreign born.

While Appalachians in Cincinnati fail to meet the legal criteria in order to receive protection under the law, it is clear that the process of achievement they experience is not the same as the process for either Cincinnati natives or white migrants from other places. While their lower educational attainments are explained by more limited resources, their lower occupational and income achievements result from different payoffs as well as different resources. Appalachians have the lowest-class backgrounds, the fewest years of education, and come from the smallest places. As a result, they do not have the resources to compete favorably with other whites. More important, the absence of these resources has more serious consequences for Appalachians than for other groups. A white migrant from some other area or a Cincinnati native who comes from a lower-class background, lacks enough years of education, or was raised on a farm still has a chance of obtaining a good job, but Appalachians must have these resources to expect to compete either for jobs or for wages.

Let us imagine that the better jobs go to people with the most years of education and the best family backgrounds, irrespective of race or ethnicity. College graduates from middle-class families can be expected to fill most of the white-collar jobs in an area. People without a college education who come from lower- and working-class families compete for the remaining positions.

The findings of this study are consistent with the interpretation that the best of those jobs go to white Cincinnati natives and migrants from other places; Appalachians are hired next; and then, if any jobs are left, blacks are employed. As a result, it is possible for other whites to achieve middle-class status without prerequisite years of education or middle-class backgrounds, but Appalachians and blacks must have those credentials if they expect to achieve.

The findings in this study further demonstrate that the failure of Appalachians in Cincinnati to achieve parity in the competition for rewards is not because they carry excess cultural baggage which causes them conflict. On the one hand, Appalachians were not found to have such cultural traits as were ascribed to them, and, on the other hand, those cultural traits did not influence the attainment process. The only reasonable hypothesis is that employers, free to choose whom they will hire, hire Appalachians only if other whites are unavailable and hire Appalachians because they prefer them to blacks. In this sense, Appalachians in Cincinnati may have been used to deny opportunities to blacks, while at the same time being denied opportunities themselves.

The evidence of separate processes of achievement demonstrates that the issue of Appalachians is more than a question of class differences. It is not that they just have less than other people. It is that they have not been given the same opportunity as other whites.

DIFFERENTIAL ASSOCIATION

If persons are members of the same group, then they are likely to associate with one another if they have such a choice. Three measures of differential association were included in the Cincinnati survey — marital partners, voluntary organizations, and neighborhoods.

Participants in the Cincinnati survey who were married were asked where their spouses had been born. Some 28 percent of the Appalachians who had married after moving to Cincinnati had married another Appalachian. This is approximately the rate which would be expected by chance alone; i.e., if Appalachians constitute about a fourth of the population and choose marital partners without regard to ethnicity, about a fourth would marry Appalachians and three-fourths would not. Appalachians, in their decisions to marry, clearly do not take into account whether the other person is also Appalachian.

There was strong evidence in the Cincinnati survey to suggest that Appalachians in voluntary organizations associate primarily with other Appalachians. Churches represent the major group in which Appalachians participate, and they choose churches which are common to Appalachia and which do not seem to attract others: 52 percent of the Appalachians were either Holiness or Baptist, while other whites were predominantly Catholic. The only other formal organization which Appalachians joined were labor unions. Appalachians did not associate in either the social, civic, or political organizations which were common to other groups in the area. The voluntary associations of Appalachians bring them into contact with other Appalachians and maintain their isolation from other people.

The notion of Appalachian neighborhoods is one of the oldest concepts in the study of Appalachian migrants. In Cincinnati, the best evidence that Appalachians tend to concentrate in neighborhoods with other Appalachians is found in Fowler's (1981) research. The Urban Appalachian Council was able to obtain information about the Appalachian backgrounds of Cincinnati schoolchildren through the Cincinnati Board of Education. Fowler's analysis of those data clearly demonstrated that Appalachians tended to cluster in particular neighborhoods of Cincinnati. While Fowler's data are more appropriate for determining neighborhood concentration, the 1975 survey analyzed

TABLE 8.1
Concentration of Appalachians in Neighborhoods

Number of Appalachians Interviewed Who Were in a Block	Cumulative Percentage of Appalachians	Cumulative Percentage of Blocks
Total sample		
Five	0	0
Four	21	6
Three	34	11
Two	68	30
One	100	67
Number	136	120
Inner city		
Five	0	0
Four	24	5
Three	31	7
Two	59	19
One	100	53
Number	49	58
Suburban		
Five	0	0
Four	18	6
Three	36	15
Two	72	40
One	100	79
Number	87	62

here supports his conclusions. Table 8.1 shows the concentration of Appalachians which was found. Interviews were collected from 120 blocks. And 21 percent of the Appalachians were found in 6 percent of the blocks, 34 percent in 11 percent of the blocks, 68 percent in 30 percent of the blocks, and 100 percent in 67 percent of the blocks. A third of the blocks had no white Appalachians. Put differently, a third of the Appalachians in this survey were found in blocks where the majority of persons interviewed were Appalachians, and another third were found in blocks which contained at least another Appalachian. If Appalachians were choosing neighborhoods at random, we would expect to find one Appalachian per block. Instead, two-thirds of the Appalachians surveyed were found in more concentrated areas.

The data further indicate that the concentration of Appalachians is almost as great in the suburbs as in the inner city. The movement of Appalachians from the inner city to the suburbs does not indicate an assimilation into the mainstream: 36 percent of suburban Appalachians and 31 percent of inner-city Appalachians lived in blocks where the majority of persons interviewed were Appalachians. They are perhaps fleeing from the inner city, but they are moving from one Appalachian neighborhood to another.

GROUP IDENTIFICATION

It is difficult to measure group identification among Appalachians because the terms used to refer to them are often derogatory in nature. The term "hillbilly," which is probably the one most frequently used, brings to mind a barefoot, uneducated, lazy man sitting on the porch, surrounded by at least six children, or off in the woods cooking mash. A person who admits to being a hillbilly is admitting to not really belonging in the city. Blacks in the United States had to struggle for many years before they adopted a name which was a symbol of pride and which people sought to identify with. The term "Appalachian" was developed by politicians and researchers and is used to identify a group of people who may identify with each other in different ways.

Participants in the Cincinnati survey were asked, "Do you think of yourself as an Appalachian?" Only 17 percent of the Appalachians surveyed identified themselves as Appalachians while 78 percent said they did not; 4 percent stated they did not know. One of the Appalachians volunteered the information that the term was one created by social workers and was being imposed upon a group of people. Clearly, Appalachians do not use that term to identify with each other.

Perhaps a different way of getting at group identification among Appalachians is to ask if they consider people's origins important. Participants were asked, "Do you think people are happier living around others who come from the same part of the country as they do?" The implication is that if they believe people are happier living around others from the same part of the country they came from, then they will seek out areas where others live who migrated from their part of the country. Indeed, 42 percent of the Appalachians said they believed people were happier living around others who came from the same part of the country. These findings suggest that Appalachians do identify with others who come from the same part of the country as they do, and that they see differential association with them as important. An even higher percentage of Appalachians with less than a high school education (55 percent) thought place of origin was important, but no differences were found between first- and second-generation migrants.

Rejection by Others

The single greatest omission in this study was the failure to ascertain how non-Appalachians felt about people from Appalachia. However, McCoy and Watkins (1981) have spent a number of years collecting jokes told in Cincinnati about Appalachians. These jokes display the stereotypes people hold about Appalachians and indicate their rejection of them as a group. They conclude that non-Appalachians living in Cincinnati hold negative stereotypes about Appalachians and apply those stereotypes indiscriminately to all persons of Appalachian origin.

The study of the socioeconomic attainment process further suggests the rejection of Appalachians by others. Appalachians were not treated in the same way as others. Those who had a good education and came from middle-class backgrounds fared well, but others, who were the vast majority, were locked out of the competition for good jobs and wages. Intentional rejection of Appalachians cannot be proven, but no evidence was found which supports any other interpretation.

SUMMARY

Eight different traits of ethnicity have been reviewed in this chapter and Appalachians showed evidence of seven of those eight. Appalachians were found to share a common origin, to have socioeconomic homogeneity, to show intergenerational inheritance, to have a separate process of achievement, to experience differential association, to identify with other Appalachians, and to experience rejection by non-Appalachians. The only attribute of an ethnic group which Appalachians lacked was the existence of unique cultural traits. In the concluding chapter, we will argue that unique cultural traits are an inappropriate criterion for the creation of ethnic groups. The conclusion that Appalachians exist as an ethnic group in Cincinnati seems obvious. What remains is to explain why they have become such a group.

9

TOWARD A THEORY OF
ETHNIC-GROUP FORMATION

For a number of years, "cultural conflict" has provided the core for explaining the presence of ethnic groups in American society. Variations on this approach hold that a given group fails to assimilate into society because it has a subculture with values which conflict with those necessary to achieve in the mainstream. Those who have applied the model to the study of Appalachians have stressed the importance of the family system and values such as independence, fatalism, and traditionalism (Weller, 1966; Giffin, 1956). At least with respect to Appalachians, this approach has hindered more than it has helped to understand the creation of an ethnic group.

First, several studies have now failed to find evidence of unique cultural values among Appalachians. Ford (1962) conducted the first survey to test the presence of values said to be characteristic of Appalachians and found no evidence of strong individualism, self-reliance, or fatalism. Instead he found a "progressive-minded, achievement-oriented" people. Dwight Billings (1974) compared attitudes of Appalachians and non-Appalachians in North Carolina and found little difference. Those differences which did exist were due to a greater percentage of Appalachians living in rural areas. Ergood (1976) measured the presence of 17 cultural characteristics among people in the Appalachian portion of Ohio and concluded that all but three of the characteristics were not descriptive of participants in his study. Finally, this study has shown that the supposedly unique characteristics of Appalachians are no more common among Appalachians than among other groups. With the exception of religious fundamentalism, Appalachians held approximately the same set of values as did others. They were not more organized around tight family groups, not more independent, not more fatalistic. Some of the supposedly Appalachian characteristics were less characteristic of Appalachians than of others. The weight of the evidence leads to the conclusion that Appalachians do not share a set of cultural values which brings them into conflict with the mainstream of society.

Second, this study has demonstrated that those cultural characteristics which supposedly hindered Appalachians were unrelated to the achievement of years of education, occupational status, or income. In most instances, persons who were more independent, more fatalistic, less trustful of institutions, or more traditionalistic did not achieve less than others. Appalachians had lower levels of achievement because they had greater limitations in their backgrounds (i.e., they more often came from a rural area, had too few years of education, and had parents who were not middle class). Those Appalachians who had those limitations suffered even more greatly than did other whites. Clearly, differences in resources and their effects were responsible for differences in achievement while cultural characteristics were unimportant.

Finally, the cultural-conflict approach has led researchers to look within the group in order to understand its failure to achieve. As William Ryan (1971) has pointed out, the underlying assumption of the cultural-conflict theory is that if a group can't compete favorably for goods and services, then that group must possess some negative trait which limits its assimilation. To solve the problem, either the group would have to change or society would have to adapt to its special needs. Such an assumption is valid only in a society where open competition exists and the only variables are those relevant to the ability to perform.

The central hypothesis of this chapter is that ethnic groups are created by the reaction of others. If other members of society group together a set of people and treat them differently than they are treated, that group will in time emerge as a subgroup. If the basis of grouping a set of people together is place of origin, then the subgroup will be an ethnic group. Perhaps this can best be understood by an illustration having nothing to do with ethnicity.

A ten-year interval separates the births of my two daughters. When my first born entered school, my wife dutifully reported for the first parent-teacher conference. To our dismay, we learned that Jessica wasn't completing her work because she spent her time talking with classmates around her. However, the teacher assured us that her work was satisfactory, considering her problem. When asked what problem she was talking about, the teacher went into a lengthy explanation of how only children needed greater interaction with peers at school since they were deprived of such stimulation at home. Such interaction hindered their learning. When asked if she had ever told Jessica to be quiet and do her work, the teacher replied that she didn't want to stunt the child's development. Only after a strong demand on my wife's part did Jessica's teacher agree to treat Jessica like she treated the other children and to tell her to settle down and do her work. Jessica was really no different from any of the other children, but the teacher decided she was and treated her differently. If that teacher's behavior had gone undetected for the year, Jessica would have learned little during the first grade and been at a permanent disadvantage in future years.

This study was designed in the cultural-conflict tradition and therefore can only suggest, but not demonstrate, how society selects a group of people and molds them into an ethnic group.

ECONOMIC PRESSURE AND ETHNIC-GROUP FORMATION

Take any ethnic classification and write down what first comes to mind about people who are members of that group. It doesn't matter what group — Irish, Polish, Italian, Jewish, Puerto Rican, Japanese — any group. Three things are probably true about the list created. First, the majority of the characteristics cited will somehow imply the unsuitability of the group. Words like hot-tempered, tightfisted, ignorant, cunning, and unscrupulous are often used in reference to different ethnic groups. To say that a person is a member of an ethnic group is to state that that person is somehow different. We are unlikely to believe that persons are superior to us because of their ethnicity. Instead, a person's ethnicity is likely to be viewed as a limitation — one that might be overcome, but a limitation nonetheless.

Second, those characteristics which are positive will often be double-edged. They will indicate something favorable about a group but still unsuitable. For example, the people may be seen as fun loving, but that of course makes them unsuitable employees since work is serious business. The people may be seen as devoted to their families, but that means they will want to leave work to visit relatives or tend to family problems, and the employer will be unable to transfer them because they will be unwilling to move away. The fact that a group is seen as hardworking may also mean that its members are only suitable for manual labor. If a group is seen as taking care of one another, they may also be seen as cliquish. Ethnic characteristics seldom conjure up only positive images of the people labeled.

McCoy and Watkins's (1981) documentation of stereotypes indicates that the same characteristics are cited about different ethnic groups. Their collection of jokes told about different groups suggests that a common set of stereotypes is applied to different groups — the particular group depends upon the area. People in cities with a Polish population tell Polish jokes; people in cities with an Irish population tell Irish jokes. They are the same jokes, only the teller and referent are different. What this implies is that ethnic groups do not have unique cultures which conflict with the dominant society. Instead, cultural characteristics are ascribed to groups by others in the area where the group resides.

The function of these ethnic classifications and cultural stereotypes is to limit competition for available goods and services in an area. For example, if there is a scarcity of jobs, employers will have several applicants for each position. Some of the applicants can be eliminated as truly unqualified; i.e., they lack necessary training and/or experience. This will still leave a pool of applicants larger than the number of available positions. Ethnic stereotypes insure that nonmembers are hired before members of the ethnic group. Although the employer may not know the applicant personally, if the former labels the applicant as a member of a particular ethnic group and believes that such people have certain undesirable traits, then that applicant will be set aside in favor of someone else.

The more the demand for goods and services and jobs exceeds the available supply, the greater the benefit will be from classifying a group of people by ethnicity and ascribing negative images to them. When a surplus of jobs exists and persons are experiencing rapid improvement in their own life styles, their origins are not likely to be seen as important. They see life improving and do not see the gain of someone else as their loss. However, when a shortage exists, a job given to one person means a job denied to someone else.

It is difficult, if not impossible, to actually determine the best qualified or the most needy in the competition for jobs or services. For example, take a position available in a widget factory. The opening is for an assembly line worker and the task is to tighten one of the bolts on the widget as it moves down the line. Training time required is about ten minutes. In a job situation of scarcity, several persons might apply for that job, any number of whom would do adequate work. There is no way to tell who would be the best workers, and if there were a way, it would cost more than it is worth, given that several choices would be adequate. In such a situation, there is no opportunity for competition based upon ability.

Given a situation where jobs are scarce and the opportunity to distinguish oneself is limited, a person benefits from being a member of the most desirable group. The greater the number of persons who can be classified in undesirable groups and the greater the number of negative images ascribed to them, the lesser the competition the individual will face. It therefore follows that the greater the scarcity of jobs in an area and the smaller the supply of goods and services, the greater will be the number of people classified by ethnicity and the stronger will be the negative images ascribed to them.

Appalachians migrated to Cincinnati at a time when the economy of the Midwest became stagnant. In the 1950s and 1960s, new industries were developing in the West, and in the 1970s, in the South. Midwestern cities faced problems of decay and a loss of jobs numbering in the thousands. People already living in those cities faced competition for fewer jobs at a time when there was a large influx of Appalachians and blacks. The classification of these people by ethnicity or race and the ascription of negative images to them eliminated them from competition with natives of the area for available jobs and services. Interestingly, migrants from areas who were not classified by ethnicity competed favorably with natives, even after other factors were taken into account. Appalachians who moved to growing cities may not have experienced the same sort of ethnic classification as Appalachians in Cincinnati have.

TARGETS OF ETHNIC-GROUP LABELING

Not all people are equally likely to be grouped together and labeled as members of ethnic groups. At least four factors are potentially important in the selection of a people.

Identifiability

In order for a people to be grouped together and classified as members of an ethnic group, outsiders must have some way in which they believe members of the group can be identified. The basis may be color, facial structure, names, language, or any other characteristic. The key to the characteristic is that it be something which distinguishes the person applying the label from those to whom the label is applied. Probably the most frequent characteristic used to label a person an Appalachian is language.

It is less important that the characteristic used to identify a group of people be accurate than that it be believed to be accurate by persons applying the label. Many persons who share the same place of origin as persons identified as members of the ethnic group may not demonstrate the characteristic in question and therefore pass as members of the group applying the label. When an accent and colloquial expressions are used to identify a person, this is particularly so. Less-educated people in general are more likely to speak in the dialect of their region. More-educated people are more frequently exposed to a greater variety of others and are more frequently trained to speak the language in its formal fashion. As a result, working-class people are more likely than middle-class people to be classified by ethnicity.

People who apply the label of ethnicity frequently regard those who pass as not possessing other characteristics of the group in question, especially those characteristics which make the person unacceptable. Appalachians, for example, who speak without an identifiable accent are probably middle class and are recognized as conducting themselves according to middle-class norms. They are viewed as having risen above the limitations of the group or as having not really been members.

The characteristic used to label a people as members of an ethnic group may cause many nonmembers to be classified as members also. Japanese in the United States, for example, are frequently identified as Chinese. Spanish-speaking people are frequently grouped together, and the label of the largest group is applied or some general term used. In New York, Mexicans may be classified as Puerto Ricans, and in Chicago, Puerto Ricans may be classified as Mexicans or the general terms Hispanic or Chicano applied, respectively. Throughout the United States, people whose origins are here are grouped together as native Americans or Indians.

The use of an accent to identify Appalachians has caused white migrants from throughout the South to be grouped with Appalachians. To those who would argue that Appalachians are a subset of southerners, let me point out that the label most frequently applied has been "hillbilly." A hillbilly is someone who lives in the mountains. People from the flatlands of Georgia, Alabama, the Carolinas, and the rest of the South are mislabeled when they are classified as hillbillies. They have been misclassified as Appalachians because outsiders cannot distinguish them by their accent, and the negative stereotypes people develop about Appalachians have been applied to those people.

Newness

Other things being equal, the newer a group of people are to an area, the more likely they are to be classified together as members of an ethnic group. If ethnic classification is a response to economic pressure, the newer the group is to the area, the more likely it is to be seen as responsible for the problems individuals are experiencing. In a stagnant economy, new migrants increase the competition for jobs simply by increasing the size of the labor force. In truth, each person who participates in the labor force increases the size of the labor force by one. However, if a shortage of jobs exists, that shortage is most likely to be attributed to the last group which entered the labor force. For example, during the recessions of the 1970s, women were frequently blamed for the shortage of jobs. Few people said it was the continued participation of men in the labor force which created the shortage. Because women entered the labor force last, they were recognized as the cause of the problem. If people who share a common origin entered the labor force recently, then they are likely to be grouped together by others in the area and labeled as an ethnic group.

Recent migrants to an area further compound blame for economic problems when they are seen as willing to work for lower wages than others are. Hostility frequently develops toward Mexicans in the West, for example, because they are believed to accept wages and work conditions others will not accept. This is believed to occur because wages are much lower in Mexico than in the United States. A Mexican can come to the United States, take a job below wage standards, and still earn more than before. In the Midwest, Appalachians could do the same thing. Morgan (1981) has demonstrated that Appalachians earned more after migration. Although this study has demonstrated that they earn less than others in Cincinnati, they still earn more than they would have earned had they not migrated. If they are willing to work for less, then they are more attractive to employers seeking to maximize profits. Ethnic classification decreases their attractiveness to employers and makes the latter more willing to pay higher wages to employ nonethnics.

Recent migrants are also more likely to be classified as members of ethnic groups because they possess most strongly the characteristics by which they are recognized. A migrant quickly learns new speech patterns and new customs which are practiced in the area of destination. Over time, it becomes difficult to differentiate them from others. Unless members of the group possess some distinctive trait which does not change over time, such as surnames or color, they will soon merge into general society.

Powerlessness

Ethnic classification will more frequently be applied to a set of people who possess little power. Because ethnic classification involves the attribution of negative characteristics to a set of people, it is important that the people classified not be able to sanction the person who labels them. If ethnic classification is an attempt to reduce competition in an area and powerful persons are labeled, they may react by denying the labeler access to goods, services, or jobs. The Jewish celebration of Purim celebrates the unsuccessful attempt of Haman to label the Jews and put them to death as unloyal to King Ahasuerus. He sought to do so in order to eliminate Mordecai as a competitor. He failed because of the power of Esther and was subsequently hanged on his own gallows.

People who are outside the economic and political mainstream of society are weaker than others and are more likely to be subjected to ethnic classification. Appalachians in Cincinnati have been particularly susceptible. They have relatively low levels of education and therefore are eliminated from competition for most middle-class jobs. Their lack of political participation means that administrators can ignore them without fear of reprisal. Because they participate in religious groups which are different from those of others and do not frequently participate in other kinds of groups, they do not develop the social networks which tie them to the mainstream. As a result, others in Cincinnati label people as Appalachians and ascribe negative characteristics to them with little fear of reprisal.

Size

People will not be grouped together by ethnicity unless a critical mass exists. Such a critical mass is necessary in order for others to attribute responsibility for economic problems to the group undergoing ethnic classification. If only a few dozen people are to be found in the area, it is difficult to convince oneself that so few matter. The group must be of sufficient size so that the person applying the ethnic label can believe the group has an impact on the supply of jobs and on the availability of goods and services in the area.

A critical mass will more quickly be reached if members of the group live in close proximity to one another and/or concentrate their employment in a few industries. In the instance of housing, if members of a group find places to live through contacts of friends and relatives, they are more likely to live close together. Outsiders will be less likely to learn about available places in the neighborhood and thus regard the fact that they can't find housing as the fault of the ethnic group. Realtors may identify the neighborhood as belonging to the ethnic group and not show available housing to nonmembers. If housing is tight, people may have difficulty finding places to live in other neighborhoods and blame the ethnic group for their problems. As a result, a few families will be held responsible for a major problem.

The tendency of outsiders to group diverse people together as members of a single ethnic group increases the probability that a critical mass will be obtained. People from Appalachia distinguish between themselves at least by state and, within states, by community. Appalachians from Tennessee do not see themselves as the same as Kentuckians. Only outsiders group them together as members of the same ethnic group. The further inclusion of non-Appalachian southerners increases the probability that a critical mass will be reached.

CULTURAL JUSTIFICATION

Americans subscribe to a norm that all persons, irrespective of race or ethnicity, should be permitted to compete for better jobs and higher wages. To deny one an opportunity to achieve on the basis of place of origin violates that norm and reflects negatively on the person who discriminates. To justify exclusion of an ethnic group, the discriminator ascribes characteristics to members of the group in the form of cultural stereotypes. An Appalachian's independence may be cited as the reason he does day labor; i.e., that way he doesn't have to tie himself down. An Appalachian's unskilled labor may be taken as evidence he likes to work with his hands or stay close to the out-of-doors. If he's unemployed, that's because he doesn't really want a steady job. He only wants to work enough to pay the rent and then to spend the rest of his time hunting and fishing.

Cultural stereotyping shifts responsibility for the failure to achieve from the discriminator to the person discriminated against. Because of their culture, members of an ethnic group may be cited as either uninterested in traditional achievement or unable to compete if they are interested. The discriminator may even hold that it isn't even the fault of the ethnic group; that that's just the culture they were born into. The discriminator then presents himself as completely willing to give members of the ethnic group an equal chance. However, such an opportunity is viewed as doomed to failure.

It isn't important that the stereotypes be accurate. It is only important that those who would sanction the discriminator accept them. When the civil rights movement was active in the South in the mid-1950s, white southerners frequently cried that northerners didn't understand what blacks were like. Frequently we heard that white southerners had a special understanding of blacks since they had lived with them all their lives. What had happened was that a shift in the control of the situation had occurred. Previously, discrimination against blacks was unbridled because local politicians who accepted the stereotypes were in control. When white liberals from the North made their influence felt, penalties were imposed for discrimination because the cultural stereotypes were not accepted.

Cultural Understanding

A by-product of cultural justification is cultural understanding. Do-gooders who have bought into the cultural-conflict perspective also cite cultural characteristics of an ethnic group as the reason for their failure to achieve. They differ from those who seek to eliminate members of an ethnic group from competition for jobs and services, in that those who would exclude members of an ethnic group use cultural characteristics to justify their discrimination. Those who support cultural understanding more frequently argue for adjustments in society which would make members of the ethnic group competitive. Different educational techniques, innovative work relationships, and other societal reforms are viewed as essential to provide members of the ethnic group a viable opportunity.

The perspective of this chapter argues that cultural conflict is a justification, rather than a cause, of the failure of members of an ethnic group to achieve in American society. Instead of developing programs which teach us that members of ethnic groups can't make it because of special problems which demand solutions, programs might be more effective if they were designed to make us aware that our cultural differences are minor and that the similarities between people are more important than their differences. Cultural explanations should not be accepted as justification for a group's failure to achieve without strong evidence that such cultural characteristics exist and equally strong evidence that they are factors in the achievement process.

Cultural Acceptance

Over time, if a group is the object of discrimination, the members of that group may develop characteristics which in fact make them unable to compete for jobs and services in the area. Members of the group may accept the argument that they possess a unique culture which is incompatible with the mainstream of society, and consequently not attempt to compete with others. If a group of people are told they possess certain traits, over time at least, some members may accept the argument and act as if such characteristics were a part of their culture, even though they are inaccurate. Just as other aspects of our self-concepts are obtained by the reactions we receive from others, so the perception that a person has certain cultural traits may be taught.

Other problems may also emerge among people excluded by society. If people try to achieve and fail through lack of an opportunity, they may become discouraged. Children will drop out of school because education will not be seen as the means to an end. Alienation will develop as people realize that the opportunity to achieve is not theirs. Once this happens, special programs will be necessary in order for these people to enter the mainstream of society, but society will have unnecessarily created the need for such solutions.

REFERENCES

Adams, James. 1971. "A series on Appalachians in Cincinnati, Ohio." *Cincinnati Post and Times-Star.*

Appalachian Regional Commission. 1977. *Appalachia – A Reference Book, First Edition.* Washington, D.C.: Appalachian Regional Commission.

———. 1979a. "The healing power of roots." *Appalachia*, 12 (May-June):37-40.

———. 1979b. *A Report to Congress on Migration.* Washington, D.C.: Appalachian Regional Commission.

Billings, Dwight. 1974. "Culture and poverty in Appalachia: a theoretical discussion and empirical analysis." *Social Forces*, 53 (December):315-23.

Blau, Peter M., and Otis Dudley Duncan. 1967. *The American Occupational Structure.* New York: Wiley.

Blum, Zahava D. 1972. "White and black careers during the first decade of labor force experience. Part II: income differences." *Social Science Research*, 1 (September):271-92.

Branscome, James. 1972. "The crises of Appalachian youth." In D. S. Walls and John D. Stephenson (eds.), *Appalachia in the Sixties.* Lexington: University Press of Kentucky, pp. 224-31.

Brown, James S. 1950. "The Social Organization of an Isolated Kentucky Mountain Neighborhood." Ph.D. dissertation, Harvard University.

———. 1968. "The family behind the migrant." *Mountain Life and Work*, 44 (September):4-7.

Brown, James S., Harry K. Schwarzweller, and Joseph J. Mangalam. 1963. "Kentucky mountain migration and the stem family: an American variation on a theme by LePlay." *Rural Sociology*, 28 (March):48-69.

Caldwell, Morris G. 1940. "The adjustments of mountain families in an urban environment." *Social Forces*, 16 (March):389-95.

Campbell, John C. 1921. *The Southern Highlander and His Homeland.* New York: Russell Sage Foundation.

Coleman, James S., Charles C. Berry, and Zahava D. Blum. 1972. "White and black careers during the first decade of labor force experience. Part III: occupational status and income together." *Social Science Research*, 1 (September):293-304.

Coleman, James S., Zahava D. Blum, Aage B. Sorensen, and Peter H. Rossi. 1972. "White and black careers during the first decade of labor force experience. Part I: occupational status." *Social Science Research*, 1 (September): 243-70.

Crowe, Martin J. 1964. "The Occupational Adaptation of a Selected Group of Eastern Kentuckians in Southern Ohio." Ph.D. dissertation, University of Kentucky.

Ergood, Bruce. 1976. "Toward a definition of Appalachia." In Bruce Ergood and Bruce E. Kuhre (eds.), *Appalachia: Social Context Past and Present*. Dubuque, Iowa: Kendall/Hunt, pp. 31-41.

Fellin, Phillip, and Eugene Litwak. 1963. "Neighborhood cohesion under conditions of mobility." *American Sociological Review*, 28 (June):364-76.

Fisher, Stephen. 1977. "Folk culture or folk tale." In J. W. Williamson (eds.), *An Appalachian Symposium*. Boone, N.C.: Appalachian State University Press, pp. 14-25.

Ford, Thomas (ed.). 1962. *The Southern Appalachian Region: A Survey*. Lexington: University Press of Kentucky.

Fowler, Gary L. 1978. "Up here and down home: Appalachians in cities." In Steven Weiland and Phillip Obermiller (eds.), *Perspectives on Urban Appalachians*. Cincinnati: Ohio Urban Appalachian Awareness Project, pp. 197-209.

———. 1981. "The residential distribution of urban Appalachians." In William W. Philliber and Clyde B. McCoy (eds.), *The Invisible Minority*. Lexington: The University Press of Kentucky, pp. 79-94.

Fox, William S., and William W. Philliber. 1975. "Racial differences in perceptions of affluence." *Sociological Focus*, 8 (October):331-42.

———. 1977. "Race, class, and perceptions of affluence." *Sociological Focus*, 10 (October):375-81.

Giffin, Roscoe. 1956. "From Cinder Hollow to Cincinnati." *Mountain Life and Work*, 32:11-20.

Gitlin, Todd, and Nanci Hollander. 1970. *Uptown: Poor Whites in Chicago*. Evanston: Harper and Row.

Gouldner, Alvin W. 1960. "The norm of reciprocity." *American Sociological Review*, 25 (February):161-78.

Hamilton, William L. 1970. *The Causes of Rural to Urban Migration among the Poor*. Cambridge: Abt Associates, Inc.

Henderson, George. 1966. "Poor southern whites: a neglected urban problem." *Journal of Secondary Education*, 41 (March):111-14.

Huelsman, Ben R. 1969. "Urban anthropology and the southern mountaineer." *Proceedings of the Indiana Academy of Science for 1968*, 78:97-103.

Isajiw, Wasvelod. 1974. "Definitions of ethnicity." *Ethnicity*, 1 (July):111-24.

Jones, Loyal. 1976. "Appalachian values." In Bruce Ergood and Bruce E. Kuhre (eds.), *Appalachia: Social Context Past and Present*. Dubuque: Kendall/Hunt, pp. 101-5.

Killian, Lewis. 1953. "The adjustment of southern white migrants to northern urban norms." *Social Forces*, 32 (October):66-9.

———. 1970. *White Southerners*. New York: Random House.

Kohn, Melvin. 1969. *Class and Conformity: A Study in Values*. Homewood, Ill.: Dorsey.

Leeds, Morton. 1971. "The process of cultural stripping and reintegration." In Americo Paredes and Ellen J. Stekert (eds.), *The Urban Experience and Folk Tradition*. Austin: University of Texas Press, pp. 165-76.

Leybourne, Grace G. 1937. "Urban adjustments of migrants from the Southern Appalachian plateaus." *Social Forces*, 16 (December):238-46.

Litwak, Eugene. 1960. "Reference group theory, bureaucratic career, and neighborhood primary-group cohesion." *Sociometry*, 23 (March):72-84.

Long, Larry. 1974. "Poverty status and receipt of welfare among migrants and nonmigrants in large cities." *American Sociological Review*, 39 (February): 46-56.

McCoy, Clyde B. and James S. Brown. 1981. "Appalachian migration to midwestern metropolitan areas." In William W. Philliber and Clyde B. McCoy (eds.), *The Invisible Minority*. Lexington: University Press of Kentucky, pp. 35-78.

McCoy, Clyde B., and Virginia McCoy Watkins. 1981. "Stereotypes of Appalachians in urban areas." In William W. Philliber and Clyde B. McCoy (eds.), *The Invisible Minority*. Lexington: University Press of Kentucky, pp. 20-31.

McKee, Dan M. and Phillip J. Obermiller. 1978. *From Mountain to Metropolis: Urban Appalachians in Ohio*. Cincinnati: Ohio Urban Appalachian Awareness Project.

Maloney, Michael E. 1974. *The Social Areas of Cincinnati: Towards an Analysis of Social Needs*. Cincinnati: Cincinnati Human Relations Commission.

———. 1978. "The implications of Appalachian culture for social welfare practice." In Steven Weiland and Phillip Obermiller (eds.), *Perspectives on Urban Appalachians*. Cincinnati: Ohio Urban Appalachian Awareness Project, pp. 253-59.

Maloney, Michael E., and Ben Huelsman. 1972. "Humanism, scientism, and southern mountaineers." *Peoples Appalachia*, 2 (July):24-27.

Miller, Tommie R. 1976. "Urban Appalachians: cultural pluralism and ethnic identity in the city." M.A. thesis, University of Cincinnati.

Montgomery, Bill. 1968. "The Uptown story." *Mountain Life and Work*, 44 (September):8-18.

Morgan, Larry C. 1981. "Economic costs and returns of Appalachian out-migration." In William W. Philliber and Clyde B. McCoy (eds.), *The Invisible Minority*. Lexington: University Press of Kentucky, pp. 115-29.

Mountain Life and Work. 1976. "Special issue: urban Appalachians." *Mountain Life and Work*, 52 (August).

Nie, Norman H., C. Hadlai Hull, Jean G. Jenkins, Karin Steinbrenner, and Dale H. Bent. 1975. *Statistical Package for the Social Sciences*. 2d ed. New York: McGraw-Hill.

Obermiller, Phillip. 1977. "Appalachians as an urban ethnic group: romanticism, renaissance, or revolution?" *Appalachian Journal*, 5 (Autumn):145-52.

Peterson, Gene B., Laure M. Sharp, and Thomas F. Drury. 1977. *Southern Newcomers to Northern Cities: Work and Social Adjustment in Cleveland*. New York: Praeger.

Philliber, William W. 1981. "Accounting for the occupational placements of Appalachian migrants." In William W. Philliber and Clyde B. McCoy (eds.), *The Invisible Minority*. Lexington: University Press of Kentucky, pp. 154-62.

Photiadis, John D. 1965. "Corollaries of Migration." *Sociological Quarterly*, 6:339-48.

_____. 1970. *Social and Sociopsychological Characteristics of West Virginians in Their Own State and in Cleveland, Ohio*. Morgantown: Appalachian Center of West Virginia University.

_____. 1975. *West Virginians in Their Own State and in Cleveland, Ohio*. Rev. ed. Morgantown: Appalachian Center of West Virginia University.

_____. 1981. "Occupational adjustments of Appalachians in Cleveland." In William W. Philliber and Clyde B. McCoy (eds.), *The Invisible Minority*. Lexington: University Press of Kentucky, pp. 140-53.

Powles, William E. 1964. "The southern Appalachian migrant: country boy turned blue collarite." In Arthur B. Shostak and William Gomberg (eds.), *Blue Collar World: Studies of the American Worker*. Englewood Cliffs: Prentice-Hall, pp. 270-81.

Reeves, Dave. 1976. "Hillbilly justice." *Mountain Life and Work*, 52 (August): 17-18.

Runciman, William G. 1966. *Relative Deprivation and Social Justice*. Berkeley: University of California Press.

Ryan, William. 1971. *Blaming the Victim*. New York: Pantheon Books.

Scanzoni, John. 1972. *Sexual Bargaining: Power Politics in the American Marriage*. Englewood Cliffs: Prentice-Hall.

Schwarzweller, Harry K. 1981. "Occupational patterns of Appalachian migrants." In William W. Philliber and Clyde B. McCoy (eds.), *The Invisible Minority*. Lexington: University Press of Kentucky, pp. 130-39.

Schwarzweller, Harry K, and James S. Brown. 1967. "Social class origins, rural-urban migration, and economic life chances: a case study." *Rural Sociology*, 32 (March):5-19.

_____. 1969. "Social structure of the contact situation: rural Appalachia and urban America." Appalachian Center. Information Report 1. West Virginia University Bulletin. Series 69, No. 12-6.

Schwarzweller, Harry K., James S. Brown, and Joseph J. Mangalam. 1971. *Mountain Families in Transition*. University Park: Pennsylvania State University Press.

Schwarzweller, Harry K., and John F. Seggar. 1967. "Kinship involvement: a factor in the adjustment of rural migrants." *Journal of Marriage and the Family*, 29 (November):662-71.

Sewell, William H. 1972. "Inequality of opportunity for higher education." *American Sociological Review*, 36 (October):793-809.

Srole, Leo. 1956. "Social integration and certain corollaries." *American Sociological Review*, 21 (December):709-16.

Sudman, Seymour. 1966. "Probability sampling with quotas." *Journal of the American Statistical Association*, 61 (September):49-71.

U.S. Bureau of the Census. 1972. *1970 Census of the Population. Alphabetical Index of Occupations and Industries*. Washington, D.C.: Government Printing Office.

Wagner, Thomas. 1975. "Urban Appalachian school children: the least understood of all." Working Paper No. 6. Cincinnati: Urban Appalachian Council.

_____. 1978. "Urban schools and Appalachian children: old values, new problems, no answers." In Steven Weiland and Phillip Obermiller (eds.), *Perspectives on Urban Appalachians*. Cincinnati: Ohio Urban Appalachian Awareness Project, pp. 269-78.

Walls, David S. 1976. "Appalachian problems are national problems." *Appalachian Journal*, 4 (Autumn):39-42.

Watkins, Virginia McCoy. 1978. "Urban Appalachian health behavior." In Steven Weiland and Phillip Obermiller (eds.), *Perspectives on Urban Appalachians*. Cincinnati: Ohio Urban Appalachian Awareness Project, pp. 288-92.

Weiland, Steven. 1978. "Twice the victims: Appalachian migrants, social services, and the urban crisis." In Steven Weiland and Phillip Obermiller (eds.), *Perspectives on Urban Appalachians*. Cincinnati: Ohio Urban Appalachian Awareness Project, pp. 5-16.

Weller, Jack E. 1966. *Yesterday's People: Life in Contemporary Appalachia*. Lexington: University of Kentucky Press.

Williams, Cratis D. 1972. "Who are the southern mountaineers?" *Appalachian Journal*, 1 (Autumn):48-56.

INDEX

ABOUT THE AUTHOR

WILLIAM W. PHILLIBER is Associate Professor of Sociology at the State University of New York at New Paltz. Until 1977 he was Associate Professor of Sociology at the University of Cincinnati.

Professor Philliber is the coeditor of *The Invisible Minority*. His articles have appeared in *Social Forces, Journal of Marriage and the Family, Sociological Quarterly, Pacific Sociological Review*, and other journals.

Professor Philliber holds a B.A. from Ouachita University, Arkadelphia, Ark., and an M.A. and a Ph.D. from Indiana University, Bloomington.